The
Once
and
Future
Wesleyan
Movement

Praise for *The Once and Future Wesleyan Movement*

"Bishop Scott Jones has spent a lifetime thinking about Wesleyan Christianity. In this important book he invites Methodists to remember who we are and where we came from and to reclaim important and oft forgotten elements of our DNA. But he also offers some very specific suggestions for what needs to change if The United Methodist Church is going to have 'a future with hope.'"
—Adam Hamilton, Senior Pastor, United Methodist Church of the Resurrection, Leawood, KS

"Articulate, incisive, and deeply compelling. Let's put a copy into the hands of every United Methodist who longs to prayerfully engage strategic holy conferencing and discern our next chapter as faith-filled Wesleyan Christians!"
—Sue Nilson Kibbey, Director, Office of Missional Church Development, West Ohio Conference, UMC

"In a time of uncertainty and change, Bishop Jones sounds the call for United Methodist leaders to recapture the dynamism and spiritual power of the Wesleyan movement that gave us birth. He invites us into conversation about changes needed for the UMC to become—once again—an innovative, cutting edge church making disciples of Jesus for the transformation of the world. *The Once and Future Wesleyan Movement* is an important, hopeful voice about the future of the UMC."
—Janice Huie, retired Bishop of the Houston Area, UMC

"Before knowing what to do, it is imperative to know who you are. This is the dilemma of the United Methodist denomination in its current moment of ferment. Bishop Scott Jones helps us to talk about right things that can move us to a future shaped by our purpose, not by our problems. This is a good conversation to join."
—Gil Rendle, Senior Vice President, Texas Methodist Foundation

"Bishop Scott Jones's new book examines current realities within and facing United Methodism by blending biblical exegesis, church history, contemporary scholarship, and the ache in his own heart to lift up—in the spirit of the Wesley's —the call to take Christianity more seriously than we have been. The good news . . . thoughtful readers will find in it an examination that can lead to innovation, transformation, and hope for a magnificent future!"
—Jim Ozier, New Church Development and Congregational Transformation, North Texas Conference, UMC

"Scott Jones has written a deeply hopeful book for the future of the Wesleyan movement. It is also practical and offers concrete and helpful paths forward. He is a gifted twenty-first-century Wesleyan leader, and this is a vision for the Wesleyan movement we need for the future!"
—L. Gregory Jones, Executive Vice President and Provost, Baylor University, Waco, TX

The
Once
and
Future
Wesleyan
Movement

Scott J. Jones

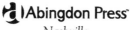Abingdon Press™
Nashville

THE ONCE AND FUTURE WESLEYAN MOVEMENT
Copyright © 2016 by Scott J. Jones

This book is printed on acid-free paper.

Library of Congress Cataloging-in-Publication Data has been requested.

ISBN: 978-1-5018-2690-0

Unless otherwise indicated, all scripture quotations are from the Common English Bible. Copyright © 2011 by the Common English Bible. All rights reserved. Used by permission. www.CommonEnglishBible.com.

All quotations from *The Works of John Wesley* are from the Bicentennial Edition (Nashville: Abingdon, 1981–).

Unless otherwise indicated all quotations from *The Book of Discipline* are from the 2012 edition (Nashville: The United Methodist Publishing House, 2012).

Quotes from *Christian Social Innovation: Renewing Wesleyan Witness* by L. Gregory Jones are copyright © 2016 by Abingdon Press, an imprint of The United Methodist Publishing House. Used by permission. All rights reserved.

The Works of John Wesley, Bicentennial Edition, volume 10 is copyright © 2011 by Abingdon Press, an imprint of The United Methodist Publishing House. Used by permission. All rights reserved.

Call to Action, copyright © 2010 by The United Methodist Publishing House. Used by permission. All rights reserved.

16 17 18 19 20 21 22 23 24 25—10 9 8 7 6 5 4 3 2 1
MANUFACTURED IN THE UNITED STATES OF AMERICA

The
Once
and
Future
Wesleyan
Movement

I am not afraid that the people called Methodists should ever cease to exist either in Europe or America. But I am afraid lest they should only exist as a dead sect, having the form of religion without the power. And this undoubtedly will be the case unless they hold fast both the doctrine, spirit, and discipline with which they first set out.

—"Thoughts upon Methodism,"
The Works of John Wesley, 9:527

Contents

Preface

A friend, who had been converted to Methodism, once referred to me as a "genetic Methodist." I took it as a compliment because it accurately describes a significant part of my identity. However, the DNA in my genes was not awakened until Albert Outler verbalized the essence of the Wesleyan movement during a class in the spring of 1978. Despite being on the road toward ordination as a fourth-generation Methodist and United Methodist preacher, I was ignorant of the doctrine and history of my own people. When Dr. Outler lectured, I suddenly discovered who I was and felt like I had arrived at my spiritual home.

Since that time I have struggled with the gap between what the Wesleyan movement was in the beginning and what it might become in the future. As a pastor, professor, and bishop, I have been given extraordinary opportunities to help shape parts of that future. This book is an attempt to assess where we are and articulate what is needed to move forward. It aims at our embodying a joyful vision of a magnificent future, while naming the obstacles that could yet prevent us from claiming all of the gifts God wants to give us.

My younger, smarter brother wrote a powerful book in early 2016. This essay deliberately seeks to build on what Gregory Jones wrote in *Christian Social Innovation: Renewing Wesleyan Witness*. Most of what he said applies to Christianity in general, and I want to be more specific about the Wesleyan movement and The United Methodist Church in particular. Thus, I will be making many references to Greg's book throughout this one. I do so with Greg's permission but without any presumption that he will agree with what I am writing.

I have borrowed the title of this book from Loren Mead's *The Once and Future Church*. That book was a wake-up call to me as a young student, and I quickly perceived how accurate his analysis was. But since the "once and future" motif was earlier used in a novel about King Arthur, applying it to the Wesleyan movement seems helpful and permissible.

As a bishop of The United Methodist Church, I am blessed with many opportunities to mobilize resources for God's purposes. I want to be faithful and fruitful, and this book is my way of thinking through the missional situation in which I serve. I pray that reading this book will stimulate the kind of conversation that leads to ever-increasingly fruitful service for Christ.

August 19, 2016
Wichita, Kansas

The Magnificent Future from a Magnificent Past

od has great things in store for the people called Wesleyans. We have a high and special calling to participate in God's mission to save the world. We have inherited wonderful resources—financial, physical, and spiritual. We have a worldwide connection that positions us to serve a diverse global village. We live in a day and age of unparalleled communication possibilities. Most important, we have a message about God, humanity, and the future of the world that is timely, relevant, and desperately needed. The world needs what Wesleyans have to offer. We have been richly blessed, and we are called to be a blessing to others.

The most important contribution we can make is to share and live the gospel with others, thereby enabling more persons—more young persons and more diverse persons—to become fully committed disciples of Jesus.

This essay seeks to describe the magnificent future that I believe God intends for Wesleyan Christians. It is written from a United Methodist perspective and assumes most of its readers are part of that significant branch of the Wesleyan movement.

I am fully committed to Wesleyan Christianity. What I am not clear about is how that movement is going to be related to The United Methodist Church. My denomination is going through incredible turmoil as several bishops and conferences challenge and disobey the fundamental ties that have held us together since 1784. At the same time, shifts in power, purpose, and opportunities mean that we cannot continue to serve Christ in the ways that worked in 1968. Thus we are in a time of deep uncertainty and rapid change.

My commitment to Wesleyan Christianity arises out of decades of study of our history, doctrine, and polity. I firmly believe that being a Wesleyan is the best way to follow Christ. I believe that the deep commitments of our polity are the best way to serve the Lord. By naming both the positives and the negatives of our present situation, I am hoping to contribute to the conversation about how Wesleyans can best lead our movement to greater faithfulness and fruitfulness in the years to come.

One reason I love the Wesleyan approach to Christianity is that we tend to downplay the more obscure parts of the gospel and Christian doctrine, focusing on what John Wesley called "practical divinity." When discussing the Methodist movement in his "Thoughts upon Methodism," he made a simple claim that serves as a brief summary of the essence of the gospel:

> What was their fundamental doctrine? That the Bible is the whole and sole rule both of Christian faith and practice.... His constant doctrine was, salvation by faith, preceded by repentance and followed by holiness.... From this short sketch of Methodism (so called) any man of understanding may easily discern that it is only plain scriptural religion, guarded by a few prudential regulations. The essence of it is holiness of heart and life; the circumstantials all point to this.[1]

By expanding on this somewhat, we can summarize Wesleyan beliefs in this way. There is a God who created the world and endowed all human beings with dignity and sacred worth. All human beings, male and female, old and young, rich and poor, of all nations, all races, all tribes, and all times and places, are valuable in God's sight. For us human beings and for our salvation, God was born as a human infant in Bethlehem two thousand years ago. Jesus of Nazareth, both fully God and fully human, taught the good news of God's reign and formed a group of followers to continue announcing his message. He died for our sins and then rose from the dead on Easter. Fifty days later the third person of the Godhead came down and empowered Christ's followers. Because of Jesus, the grace of God is active in the life of every human being, even before he or she is aware of it. That grace convinces us of our sin. God's grace next justifies those who are willing to accept God's offer of salvation. Those persons who believe in Christ as Lord and Savior are then baptized into Christ's body and they join the church. It is through the ministry of the church that most people have access to the saving grace of God. That grace comes through worship, Bible study, prayer, holy communion, baptism, and small-group conversation. Through the church's ministries and as individuals, disciples are actively transforming the world to be more in accord with God's will for justice, healing, and salvation for all people. As disciples practice these means of grace, God sanctifies them to be more and more holy, more and more like Jesus. This way of life is called "eternal life" in the Bible and leads to life with God in heaven after death.

At our best, Wesleyans are always asking how the Christian faith affects daily life and what practices will help us make progress on our spiritual journey. At the same time, we have sought to bring our Christian faith to bear on the communities and nations in which we live so that we are used by God to heal the sick, teach the young, and bring justice to the oppressed.

There are many different Christian churches actively sharing this good news about a saving way of life with people all over the world. Some of them are Wesleyan churches separate from The United Methodist Church. Others are historically from different branches of the Christian movement. But Wesleyans engage in this gospel ministry with several particular emphases:

- A focus on God's grace, rooted in the love of God for all persons

- A connection for common action, "organizing to beat the devil"[2]

- A practical focus that gives priority to concerns about living the Christian life

- A willingness to embrace other Christian groups as sisters and brothers

- A worldwide denomination with organic unity of churches on four continents

Wesleyans are not alone in serving God's purposes in these ways, but we have a distinctive approach that should not be neglected.

Yet, far too often, United Methodists participate in the malaise that seems to be affecting so much of world culture at the beginning of a new millennium. My brother, Gregory Jones, opened his recent book *Christian Social Innovation: Renewing Wesleyan Witness* with this provocative sentence: "Most people are hungry for innovation." He continues,

> We are hungry for new ways of living and doing things that can chart better paths forward. We are hungry for innovation because we know that we are facing challenges that are "complex," problems that are "wicked." . . . We have a looming sense that too much of our world is in a state of degeneration, that older institutions and patterns of life are decaying and dying. We have a sense that we need something new.[3]

The "sense that we need something new" is widespread in American culture. The malaise and desire for God to do a new thing among us is widespread in American United Methodism as well. We have been declining in membership and worship attendance for almost fifty years. We have been aging, and our sense of importance in American society has diminished.

In my brother's book he relates a conversation he had with his colleague at Duke University, Greg Dees. Dees was the founder of the social entrepreneurship movement who described social entrepreneurs as change agents in the social sector. Among other things Dees says they are known for their missions to create social value, relentless pursuit of their mission, and continuous learning. They act boldly and focus on helping their constituencies and creating good outcomes.[4]

My brother then says,

> In reading this list, it struck me: these characteristics describe the Wesleyan revival in eighteenth-century England and the vitality of Wesleyan movements in the nineteenth and early twentieth centuries in the United States and, more recently, in other parts of the world (especially Africa). Even more, these characteristics describe most Christian renewal movements throughout the history of the Church. This awareness led me to the rediscovery of a Christian vision of social innovation.[5]

Greg Jones then relates a lunch-time conversation with Dees that started with the question "What happened to the Church?" After a request for clarification, Dees said,

> I am curious why the Church lost interest in entrepreneurial approaches to social needs and problems. For most of American history, faith-based communities led the way in innova-

tive approaches in sectors such as education, health, housing, food, just to name a few. This was particularly true when you think about approaches that achieved scale and scope: faith-based hospitals and hospices, colleges and universities founded by Christians, organizations such as Salvation Army, Habitat for Humanity, and World Vision.

Yet it seems that about forty to fifty years ago, faith-based communities lost interest in what we now call social entrepreneurship. The field I am now associated with, social entrepreneurship, emerged in business schools in part because of the decline of interest by the Church. And so I wonder, what happened to the Church?[6]

The question haunted my brother and haunts me. Greg Jones offers two answers with which I agree. First, he says we have forgotten who we are. My own faith story illustrates the ways in which active United Methodists no longer know our history and our doctrine and thus cannot articulate our identity. I am a fourth-generation Methodist and then United Methodist preacher. Yet I had never heard the hymn "Amazing Grace" until 1970 when Judy Collins recorded it as a popular song. While in college, I was invited to lunch by my advisor in the philosophy department at the University of Kansas. He was a practicing Presbyterian layman and knew I was headed to seminary. He said, "As a Methodist, you must believe in the warmed heart." I was confused and did not know what to say. As a twenty-two-year-old college senior, I had never heard about John Wesley's Aldersgate experience of having his heart "strangely warmed." My professor then explained a little of my own spiritual heritage to me. He knew Methodism better than I did. Fortunately for me, during the first year of my seminary education I enrolled in a class on Wesley and the Wesleyan tradition taught by Albert Outler. When Dr. Outler lectured, I realized that he was describing who I was and what I wanted to believe. To my amazement, I discovered that this Wesleyan approach to Christian life and beliefs was actually the official doctrine of the denomination. Yet in all my years of listening to leaders of the church preach and teach, very little of the Wesleyan understanding of the way of salvation had ever been communicated.

After talking with many other people, I came to understand that my story was quite common. Just at the time when our culture was becoming more and more secularized and when other religious options were becoming more readily available, United Methodism quit teaching our own tradition and beliefs. Our great success in the 1950s had lulled us into complacency. Like children who inherit wealth created by an earlier generation, we came to believe that we did not need to create new wealth and that we could spend down our inheritance without checking the balance in the account. We lived off the shell of our past success without attending to its deep roots.

The second cause my brother identified is that we turned inward. I have long said that too many congregations have become clubs that exist for the benefit of their members. I have often asked churches to tell me their mission statement. Most of the time, the response is similar to "I know we have one, but I cannot tell you what it is." But in one case a church member told me his church's mission without quoting an official statement. It was a congregation that had been served for forty years by student pastors from the nearby seminary. This leader said, "Our church's purpose is to keep the building open for weddings and funerals and to help young pastors learn how to be real ministers in their next appointment." Unfortunately, the only unusual aspect of this statement is that the leader was able to verbalize it clearly. For many congregations their goal is to take care of the persons who are already members. When new people move to town, they are not invited or welcomed to join. When there are children who are not related to members, they are not given scholarships to camp. Especially when the neighborhood is changing to include members of a different ethnic group, the congregation finds ways to make sure that "those newcomers" cannot use the facilities.

This contrasts with the concept that mission, including evangelism, is essential to the identity and nature of the church. Thus, an inward-facing congregation that refuses to offer Christ to its community is, to that extent, really not a church.

This same inwardness has infected our denomination in two ways. The first is encapsulated in a comment made by a consultant working with the Call to Action process in 2010. He said to one of the participants, "The trouble with you Methodists is that you believe if you have gone to a meeting, you have done something." Many times we are so preoccupied with procedures, gatherings, and status that we fail to measure whether any fruit was produced. We have developed a number of litmus tests that have nothing to do with making disciples of Jesus Christ for the transformation of the world. Whenever they predominate, our conferences and agencies have turned inward rather than outward.

Second, too many of our churches have focused on taking care of their members rather than engaging outsiders in discussions about following Jesus. In 2015, 51 percent of the congregations in the Great Plains Conference experienced no new professions of faith. That means that they did not even have a confirmation class. Unfortunately, this was an increase of 4 percentage points over the 2014 numbers. When a district superintendent was urging her pastors to help persons come to Christ and profess their faith, one brave clergyperson said in front of all her district colleagues, "If professions of faith are important, someone should teach us how to do them." Too many of our local churches, conferences, and agencies care more about taking care of existing staff and members rather than measuring professions of faith, worship attendance, and persons moved out of poverty.

The corollary to this inward focus is that too many of us are no longer asking how God can use us to transform the world. The point to Dees's question, "What happened to the Church?" is that we Christians are no longer thinking about innovative solutions to the problems facing the world. Greg Jones states,

> It is crucial for the Church's own internal integrity and witness that we rediscover a vision for social innovation and entrepreneurship. We need to recover this witness not so we might be relevant, but rather as an intrinsic part of our witness to the God whom we believe is making all things new by

the power of the Holy Spirit. Ironically the best way we can become relevant is not by focusing on how to be relevant, but rather by rediscovering and renewing our own mission and purpose. . . .

I worry that faith-based organizations, including churches, might not endure, much less flourish, unless they reconnect with social entrepreneurship mindsets, skills, and virtues.[7]

What would it take to become an innovative, cutting-edge church?

United Methodists have inherited vast resources built up over more than two centuries. We have many elements that would be helpful for dynamic ministry that is both faithful and fruitful in the twenty-first century. Many different prescriptions have been offered, and the deepest and most important one was offered by Bishop Janice Huie. When she began her service as president of the Council of Bishops, she gave an address to the council. In that address she called for The United Methodist Church to once again become a movement. I think she is absolutely right.

Her address stimulated a lot of conversation among bishops about what it means to become a movement once again. I heard some agree with Bishop Huie and then contrast being a movement rather than an institution. I heard this from people whose whole ministry, including their authority and opportunities for effecting change (in addition to their salaries, office expenses, and pensions), was cared for by the institutional side of The United Methodist Church. Somehow the desire to be a movement at the expense of being an institution did not sound right coming from such leaders.

My both/and approach to theology, expressed as "the extreme center," says that the dichotomy between these two is a false one. Beginning in the 1960s, many people seeking change in society used the word *institution* and its cognates in negative ways. Fresh, new, creative approaches were called for, and stable patterns of behavior with rules and expectations were denigrated.

The problem with this is that any successful movement must become institutionalized over time in order to survive. In order to accomplish its goals, a movement must answer various questions about how leaders are chosen, how decisions are made, how resources are allocated, and how membership in the group is recognized. Answers to these questions can be developed in the movement stage, but once answered, they form the basis of the institution. Future expectations are built upon those answers, and when new questions arise there are new answers given. In short, successful movements become institutions.

This is true of churches as well. David Bosch, in his *Transforming Mission*, evaluates the transition from the earliest phase of the Christian movement to the next one. He writes,

> First, we have to ask whether it is fair to expect a movement to survive only as a movement. Either the movement disintegrates or it becomes an institution—this is simply a sociological law. Every religious group that started out as a movement and managed to survive, did so because it was gradually institutionalized: the Waldensians, the Moravians, the Quakers, the Pentecostals and many more. The same was bound to happen to the early Christian movement. It could not, in the

long run, survive merely in the shape of a charismatic leader with his band of lower-class artisans from the periphery of society. Actually, it probably took that form only during the first months of Jesus public ministry. . . . Be this as it may, the Josephs and Nicodemuses helped to smooth the transition from a charismatic movement to a religious institution. In this way they also helped to guarantee the survival of the movement. Without that, and speaking humanly and sociologically, the Jesus movement would perhaps have been absorbed into Judaism or have disappeared, "leaving but a vague souvenir of a bizarre, millennial movement."[8]

Greg Jones points to an earlier development in the history of Israel, recorded in the book of Numbers:

The census, the Meeting Tent instructions, the different roles of Israel's tribes and the rules they follow—together they are the structural embodiment of what it means to be Israel—to be a people made holy, to be a blessing to the world and a witness to Yahweh's reign. Institution building isn't a necessary evil; it is integral to their identity as a people; it is the structural pattern of who they are, and a sign of blessing. To be Israel means to be organized in just this way. Institution building is identity building.[9]

The same is true of Methodism. During the latter years of his life, Wesley made provision for the institutional continuation of the Methodist movement. He ordained Richard Whatcoat and Thomas Vesey for work in America and set apart Thomas Coke as General Superintendent. He created the Legal

Hundred and provided for the continuation of Methodism in Britain. He knew that Methodism had more work to do after his death, and he provided institutional forms to insure that the ministry would continue. The power of the Wesleyan movement was channeled into institutional forms.

Bishop Huie's point in her speech was not to destroy the institution. No one is suggesting we get rid of our assets and start from nothing like we did in the eighteenth century. At the same time we need to recapture the dynamism and spiritual power of being a movement. In short, we need to become a movemental institution. We must embrace both sides of this dichotomy.

The two most important characteristics of a movemental institution are clarity of purpose and discipline in execution.

Our church took a giant step in the right direction in 1996 when the General Conference adopted a new mission statement. It has been amended twice, most recently at the 2012 General Conference. In the 2016 *Book of Discipline*, its opening sentences will say, "*The Mission*—The mission of the Church is to make disciples of Jesus Christ for the transformation of the world. Local churches and extension ministries of the Church provide the most significant arenas through which disciple-making occurs."[10]

While these two short sentences are widely quoted throughout the church, the mission statement actually continues through ¶122. There the process of disciple-making is summarized by five phrases:

- Proclaim the gospel
- Lead persons to commit their lives to God

- Nurture persons in Christian living
- Send persons into the world to live lovingly and justly
- Continue the mission of seeking, welcoming, and gathering persons into the community of the body of Christ

The study of The United Methodist Church completed by the Towers-Watson firm in 2011 noted that while the mission statement was widely quoted, there was no consensus about what *disciple-making* meant. Indeed, when many persons are asked what it means to make disciples of Jesus Christ for the transformation of the world, they often state that they don't know what it would look like.

In fact, the addition of the phrase "for the transformation of the world" added nothing to the content of the mission statement if it was considered in its entirety. However, many people interpreted "making disciples" to include only evangelism, and they wanted some indication of social justice in the easily repeatable first sentence. Again, though, a full understanding of "transformation of the world" would also include evangelism because the world will not be in accordance with God's will until

> at the name of Jesus everyone
> > in heaven, on earth, and under the earth might bow
> and every tongue confess that
> > Jesus Christ is Lord, to the glory of God the Father
> > (Phil 2:10-11)

Yet, the adoption of the 1996 mission statement has changed the conversation throughout the church and provided a rallying point for self-evaluation. Gil Rendle, author of *Wandering in the Wilderness*, has said that the adoption of this statement was the most important action in the recent history of the UMC. It changed our focus—as pastors, as lay leaders, and as bishops—from making members to making disciples. The problem was that everything he had learned in his early ministry was about helping people become good members of an institution.[11]

The deep reality of our mission statement is that it is rooted in both the Great Commission of Matthew 28 and our doctrine as United Methodist Christians. Our Wesleyan doctrine emphasizes the power of God's grace to change lives.

- Prevenient grace affirms people as they are because the love of God is universal and gives dignity and value to every person regardless of gender, race, ethnicity, tribe, language group, or national identity.

- Convincing grace helps us confront our sin and recognize our need for God. It leads us to repentance and seeking salvation through faith alone.

- Justifying grace brings us to say yes to God's offer that we might be God's sons and daughters, to accept Christ as Lord and Savior, and to become Jesus's disciples. It is the entry point into the Christian life, building on all of the gracious activity that has gone before.

- Sanctifying grace leads to spiritual growth in our faith, our hope, and our love, always "[fixing] our eyes on Jesus, faith's pioneer and perfecter" (Heb 12:2).

- At every step the means of grace—worship, Bible study, prayer, holy communion, baptism, Christian conferenc-

ing, ministry with the poor—provide the ordinary channels through which God's amazing grace transform lives
and leads them on the way of salvation.

Yet, in the cacophony of influences present in modern culture, this way of life is only one small voice among many that
clamor for attention from our people. If this is the gospel as
understood by Wesleyan Christians, how are we to preach and
live it so that it gets heard?

With regard to disciplined execution, we have a lot of
room for improvement. Speaking in general terms about what
is needed, Greg Jones names it as "traditioned innovation." He
describes it this way:

> Traditioned innovation is a way of thinking and living that
> holds the past and future together in creative tension; a habit
> of being that depends on wise judgment, requiring both a
> deep fidelity to the patterns of the past that have borne us to
> the present and a radical openness to the changes that will
> carry us forward. Our feet are firmly on the ground with our
> hands open to the future.[12]

The question facing Wesleyan Christians today is how we
can best serve Christ out of our tradition. Faithfulness to the
tradition many times means the kind of innovation that our
foremothers and forefathers used in their times and places. The
Wesleyan movement should be a living tradition that stays true
to its core values while adapting to changing circumstances.
We should not be frozen in time, woodenly repeating what
worked 50 or 150 years ago. As Jaroslav Pelikan made clear:

"Tradition is the living faith of the dead, traditionalism is the dead faith of the living."[13]

This book is about discerning the core of the Wesleyan movement and considering how it might innovate for its future faithfulness and fruitfulness.

Key Questions

To discern the magnificent future God has in store for our movement, Wesleyans need to ask some key questions about our past and present. While the next few years are uncertain, Christianity has faced similar challenges in the past, and we need to harvest resources from our foremothers and forefathers that can help us face our challenges today. While we "run the race that is laid out in front of us" and because "we have such a great cloud of witnesses surrounding us," we can "throw off any extra baggage, get rid of the sin that trips us up, and fix our eyes on Jesus, faith's pioneer and perfecter" (Heb 12:1-2). Sometimes our ancestors invented new approaches to be faithful to Christ. We can and should learn from them.

Many such questions could be listed, but understanding some important truths about each of these will inform a vision of what the Wesleyan movement might become.

What Should We Learn from Our Christian Past?

From the early 300s in the Christian era to the middle of the twentieth century, Christianity occupied a privileged place in the culture of Europe and eventually in North America. The history of how the church in all of its various forms interacted with governments, societal institutions, and other entities in all of their various forms, is complex. But it is generally accurate to say that Christianity was a dominant force that enjoyed widespread cultural influence down through the centuries. Western culture was, in many significant respects, a Christian culture until recently.

In many countries for many centuries, the Christian church was established and in a symbiotic relationship with the state. Emperors were crowned by popes, kings and queens were crowned by archbishops, and it was assumed that every citizen of the country was also a Christian. The state protected the church, and the church provided moral legitimacy for the state. There was widespread consensus that Christianity was an important part of the glue holding together the people, the culture, and the empire or nation.

Christian churches still have some degree of continuing influence in Europe and North America. However, many scholars have noted that from being established as the official religion of most European countries, Christianity has changed to being one of many religious options. We can learn important lessons from two important periods in our Christian past: the formative years of the early Christian movement and the formative years of the early Wesleyan movement.

But there were almost three centuries of time in which Christianity was not so influential and privileged. Early Christianity was small and marginalized. From Jesus's ascension to the early 300s, Christianity in the Roman Empire was serving God in a multireligious, multiethnic empire with a government that was sometimes hostile and sometimes indifferent.

Prior to Constantine, Christianity was one of many religions in the Roman Empire. While Judaism was the dominant religion in Palestine, there were many different expressions of Judaism, and the destruction of the temple in 70 CE made those divisions even more distinct. Elsewhere in the empire, the worship of the gods and goddesses of Greek and Roman religion was organized. The worship of Mithras, with elaborate ceremonies, was popular through the empire. Manichaeism was a dualistic religion that spread during the third century. For almost three hundred years, Christianity functioned as one religious option among many. It did not have the privileges of government support. Indeed, it went through periods of persecution and government harassment.

Kavin Rowe, in his *World Upside Down: Reading Acts in the Graeco-Roman Age*, makes the point that religion in all its forms in the Roman Empire included all aspects of one's life. He notes that in the ancient world, culture was inseparable from religion. He writes,

> Converting to the God of the Christians was not merely an adjustment of this or that aspect of an otherwise unaltered

basic cultural pattern; rather, worshipping the God of the Christians simultaneously involved (1) an extraction or removal from constitutive aspects of pagan culture (e.g., sacrifice to the gods), and (2) a concomitant cultural profile that rendered Christians identifiable as a group of outsiders. Yet the practices that created this cultural profile were themselves dependent upon the identity of God. Christian ecclesial life, in other words, was the cultural explication of God's identity.[1]

The world in which Christianity was born and developed was one in which many different religions were competing for the attention and loyalty of the people, and the choice of religion determined one's community and way of life.

A Christian apologist named Aristides wrote to the emperor Hadrian, trying to give a positive description of his people. It portrays Christianity at its best as he saw it:

> They love one another, and from widows they do not turn away their esteem; and they deliver the orphan from him who treats him harshly. And he, who has, gives to him who has not, without boasting. And when they see a stranger, they take him in to their homes and rejoice over him as a very brother; for they do not call them brethren after the flesh, but brethren after the spirit and in God.[2]

Loren Mead, in his *Once and Future Church*, reminds us that before Constantine became emperor, the church was operating in a cultural context that has many parallels to Western culture today. Building on various scholars who talk about the disestablishment of American Christianity, Mead argued that we should look to the early church as a model. Christendom, inaugurated by Constantine, is dead.

Mead notes that in order to survive, Christianity had to have clear boundaries between its community and those outside. Being a Christian meant you were not a follower of another religion. Your community was composed of those who followed Jesus, and it defined the contours of the believer's entire life.

Rowe's analysis of the book of Acts draws attention to the ways in which Christianity as a way of life, based in a community, was in significant conflict with its cultural context. He writes,

> Through its discussion of the Christian missionaries' encounter with the constitutive aspects of pagan culture in Lystra, Philippi, Athens and Ephesus, chapter 2 traced the profound collision between the Christian mission and the wider Graeco-Roman world that accompanies the missionaries' call to repentance, forgiveness, and communal formation. In Lystra, where Paul and Barnabas were taken as gods, the entire complex of pagan piety that entailed the divinizing of human beings and the traditional practice of sacrifice to the gods was rebuffed, criticized, and labeled "empty." In its place the Christian missionaries proclaimed the necessity for a "turn" to "the living God." ... Taken as a whole, these reactions express narratively the fact that the "good news" seemed far from good to many it encountered; instead it entailed a deep threat to preexisting, foundational ways of life in the Mediterranean world.[3]

Rowe's discussion shows how the conflicts described in Acts are the opening events in the deep cultural challenge that Christianity faced in the Roman Empire. How can they faithfully live in a pagan culture?

The Wesleyan movement in the twenty-first century faces a cultural situation that has some parallels with the first three centuries. America and Europe are becoming much more secularized, and the privileged position of Christianity is rapidly disappearing. Instead of establishment, Christians are experiencing overt hostility from academia, the entertainment industry, media, and other powerful forces that shape our culture. No longer do public schools engage in corporate prayer. No longer do communities protect Wednesday night and Sunday morning for church events. No longer is a church affiliation seen as a requirement for a successful business career.

The most important learning from the early church is that being a disciple of Jesus must have clear identifying characteristics and behaviors that distinguish Christians from nonbelievers. We can no longer treat membership in the church as if it were just one more club or civic organization to whom we paid nominal dues and attended the annual meeting. It can no longer be a tribal identifier to show something of our ancestry but nothing of our current priorities.

This will be a wrenching change for many United Methodist members and congregations. The cultural captivity of the church has meant that people believe they are good United Methodist Christians if they are baptized and confirmed, attend worship once a year, contribute a few dollars occasionally, and self-identify as United Methodists. Their church affiliation entitles them to use the building for life-changing events such as marriages and funerals, but it does not direct their daily and weekly thoughts and actions. These are nominal Christians, not fully devoted followers of Jesus.

The future of the Wesleyan movement I am trying to describe in this book depends on a radical reorientation of church away from this cultural captivity to a deeper discipleship. As one of our congregations puts it in their mission statement, we need to be "calling the 'Christian-ish' to become passionate servants of Christ."[4] But such a new orientation means that Christians are going to be identifiably distinguished from non-believers in the larger culture. We will have to gain extraordinary clarity about what it means to be a "passionate servant of Christ" and then develop processes and patterns for assisting persons to live their lives on that journey.

The similarity with the early church context also extends to the presence of other religions in the culture. When Paul was preaching in Athens he reached out to the worshippers of other gods and sought to connect with an opening he saw in their worship practice. He said, "As I was walking through town and carefully observing your objects of worship, I even found an altar with this inscription: 'To an unknown God.' What you worship as unknown, I now proclaim to you" (Acts 17:23). Until recently, the religious options for Americans were limited to the various expressions of Christianity and Judaism. Since 1960, the number of practitioners of other religions, the development of new religions, and the rise of those who have no religious affiliation (the "nones") have created a new environment. Our mission field has changed.

Someone who is seeking a relationship with the divine has a wide variety of options from which to choose. While many religious people seek to minimize competition, there is a sense in which each form of Christianity is making a claim to offer the right approach to "the way, the truth, and the life." For many years the competition was between the different denominations of Christianity. Now, Christians are more likely to perceive their common aspects while recognizing that the religious marketplace is much more crowded. The similarity with the Graeco-Roman Empire is strong.

But there is a limit to the "once and future church" analogy with the pre-Constantinian period. Specifically, that period was a pre-Christian culture during which the philosophers in Athens could say about Paul that "he seems to be a proclaimer of foreign gods" (Acts 17:18). Our time is post-Christian, during which the philosophical and theological claims about God, the world, and humanity have been discussed and debated for two millennia. One professor of evangelism in the United Kingdom said to me that the process of British secularization had gone so far in his country that few people were open to hearing about Jesus as the incarnate son of God who died to save our souls. He said, "People are more open to the possibility that God is a yellow banana than that God was in Christ reconciling the world to himself."

The challenge we are facing today is that the role of religion in the culture is changing, and the gospel must be adapted to a new context. For help in this matter, we can look to the evangelical revival of the eighteenth and nineteenth centuries. As industrialization and urbanization gathered steam in Great Britain, people were leaving rural life and moving to the cities. The old ways in which religion and community life formed a coherent whole were being disrupted and new forms of community were needed. Furthermore, intellectual challenges from the rise of modern science and the challenges of deism meant that old patterns of Christian teaching were more and more suspect.

John Wesley, Charles Wesley, George Whitfield, Howell Harris, and several other clergy in England and Wales experienced significant conversions in the first half of the eighteenth century. They reconnected with the evangelical doctrines of the Church of England and set out to change the practice of nominal Christianity into deeper discipleship. John Wesley preached three sermons before the University of Oxford decrying the shallow faith and sporadic practice of the official religion of the university. Methodist historiography has given too much credence to Wesley's caricature of the lack of religious faith at the university, but the Wesleys were clearly calling men and women of eighteenth-century Britain to take Christianity more seriously than they were. John said,

> Is this city a *Christian* city? Is Christianity, *scriptural* Christianity, found here? Are we, considered as a community of men, so "filled with the Holy Ghost," as to enjoy in our hearts, and show forth in our lives, the genuine fruits of that Spirit? Are all the magistrates, all heads and governors of colleges and

halls, and their respective societies (not to speak of the inhabitants of the town), "of one heart and one soul"? Is "the love of God shed abroad in our hearts"? Are our tempers the same that were in him? And are our lives agreeable thereto? Are we "holy as he who hath called us is holy in all manner of conversation"?[5]

Wesley's critique of his contemporary Christianity was overstated, and yet he was calling his country to a deeper commitment and more disciplined practice of the faith. It was a time for a revival of basic Christianity because the demographic and cultural realities were changing. Demographically, people were leaving rural areas and migrating to the cities. Culturally, a number of factors were changing the patterns of life experienced by the lower classes.

A crucial task in the demographic changes of the time was the ability to form new Christian communities. In places where the Church of England was strong, it remained strong. But in the places where the population was growing because of demographic shifts, Methodism took hold and helped people build new forms of religious community to adapt to their new way of life.

Among the evangelicals, the Wesleys were the most effective in creating those communities and linking them together in supportive networks. John and Charles learned a great deal from the Pietist movement in Germany about the importance of religious societies. Others in Great Britain were forming such societies as well. Then they stumbled across the class meeting as the most important place in which new believers were disciple during the eighteenth-century revival.

David Hempton's analysis of Methodism in the eighteenth century notes that where the Church of England was strong, notably in the southeast of England, Methodism made only modest gains. The Wesleyan movement demonstrated a greater capacity than Anglicanism

> to adapt to the changing conditions of a new world order. . . . Its greatest gains came in the large, dispersed parishes of Wales and the north of England where demographic expansion and pastoral neglect offered new openings for the itinerant foot soldiers of the Methodist army. It was at the Anglican interface with mobility and change that Methodism made its conquests.[6]

That ability to spread the gospel and take advantage of people's mobility and the changes in culture was even more evident in the newly independent colonies in America. The adoption of the United States Constitution in 1789 followed quickly by the Bill of Rights enshrined the principle of religious freedom for the new country. Churches that had been culturally dominant in each of the colonies—some by establishment and with tax support—were suddenly faced with competition from other Christian groups. As America expanded across the Allegheny Mountains, the settlement of new areas by Euro-Americans offered new patterns of Christian allegiance.

Into this very fluid situation came the Methodists and other upstart denominations. Nathan Hatch, in his *Democratization of American Christianity*, describes the process by which the established churches were unprepared for the new cultural competition. Hatch argues that the theme of democratization is central to understanding the development of American Christianity and that the changes in religious life were crucial in the shaping of the young American republic. He writes,

> The wave of popular religious movements that broke upon the United States in the half century after independence did more to Christianize American society than anything before or since. Nothing makes that point more clearly than the growth of Methodist and Baptist movements among white and black Americans. Starting from scratch just prior to the Revolution, Methodism in America grew at a rate that terrified other more established denominations. By 1820 Methodist membership numbered a quarter million; by 1830 it was twice that number. Baptist membership multiplied tenfold in the three decades after the Revolution; the number of churches increased from five hundred to over twenty-five hundred. The black church in American was born amidst the crushing vigor of these movements and quickly assumed its own distinct character and broad appeal. By the middle of the nineteenth century, Methodist and Baptist churches had splintered into a score of separate denominations, white and black. In total these movements eventually constituted two-thirds of the Protestant ministers and church members in the United States.[7]

While this was going on, more established denominations such as Congregationalists, Presbyterians, and Episcopalians were stunned at the numerical success of these upstart movements. They were at first unable or unwilling to adapt to the new culture and the accompanying demographic changes. Eventually, they were changed by the success of the new movements and adopted camp meetings and other new measures of reaching people.

Two important lessons can be learned from the early church period and early Methodism. The first is that adaptation to a new cultural reality is possible and in fact was done by our foremothers and forefathers. There are times when we feel discouraged because recent trends have not been favorable. While our faith in God should strengthen us and give us a wider perspective, it also helps to see that God has led his people through difficult times before and that God's purposes have been accomplished.

The second lesson to be learned is that missional effectiveness requires both a focus on the basics of the faith and a willingness to adapt to new circumstances and opportunities. This process began at the Jerusalem Council, whose work is described in Acts 15. The leaders of the church were faced with the outpouring of the Holy Spirit on the Gentiles, and they had to decide how the Jewish movement following Jesus as Messiah might be adapted to this new opportunity. They knew that these persons were Christians, but they had to figure out how to protect the essence of Jesus's teachings about discipleship. They developed the key distinction between different parts of the law, saying that some parts were not required of Gentile converts while other parts were binding on all of Jesus's disciples. Later described as distinguishing the ceremonial and moral parts of the law, the clarification allowed for including Gentiles in table fellowship while protecting the aspects of Jesus's teaching that were most central to his ministry. During the next three centuries, Christians learned to navigate allegiance to Jesus as king while living peaceably in the Roman Empire.

The Methodist revival in the eighteenth and nineteenth centuries was a time of focusing on the basics of Christianity and letting go of practices that no longer served the church's mission well. Innovations such as field preaching, class meetings, itinerancy, conference, and lay preachers helped replace a system of episcopacy and parishes that was not well suited to the emerging industrial culture of Great Britain. In the context of Euro-American expansion across America, Methodism's discipline and flexibility gave it distinct advantages over other forms of Christianity. But it was Methodism's focus on the essence of the gospel and their willingness to try new means that allowed them to be successful.

What Do We Need to Know about the Current Context of American Christianity?

Three scholars have outlined five important changes in American culture that shaped the mission field for the Wesleyan movement. While there are many such books seeking to capture the deep changes we are all experiencing, these three scholars offer deep insights into key trends in America today. From these trends we can draw conclusions about how the Wesleyan movement might address current problems and opportunities.

Robert Putnam in his *Bowling Alone: The Collapse and Revival of American Community* describes the value of social capital—connections among individuals and their social networks. He argues that social capital is both a private good and a public good and that it both bonds people together in groups and bridges across social dividing lines. He analyzes political participation, civic participation, religious participation, connections in the workplace, informal social connections, altruism, volunteering, philanthropy, reciprocity, honesty, and trust with the tools of a social scientist. He looks for data that indicates the trends of relationships. He acknowledges that some trends have been positive. However, he draws the following conclusion:

> By virtually every conceivable measure, social capital has eroded steadily and sometimes dramatically over the past two generations. The quantitative evidence is overwhelming, yet most Americans did not need to see charts and graphs to know that something bad has been happening in their communities and in their country. Americans have had a growing sense at some visceral level of disintegrating social bonds.[8]

Yet, he is hopeful about the future. Drawing on lessons from the early twentieth century, he suggests a number of ways in which community might be revived in the early twenty-first century. He writes,

Just as did our predecessors in the Progressive Era, we need to create new structures and policies (public and private) to facilitate renewed civic engagement. As I shall explain in more detail in a moment, leaders and activists in every sphere of American life must seek innovative ways to respond to the eroding effectiveness of the civic institutions and practices that we inherited. . . .

Faith-based communities remain such a crucial reservoir of social capital in American that it is hard to see how we could redress the erosion of the last several decades without a major religious contribution. . . .

So I challenge America's clergy, lay leaders, theologians, and ordinary worshipers: Let us spur a new, pluralistic, socially responsible "great awakening," so that by 2010 Americans will be more deeply engaged than we are today in one or another spiritual community of meaning, while at the same time becoming more tolerant of the faiths and practices of other Americans.[9]

When speaking in Lawrence Kansas a number of years ago, Putnam made a similar point, saying, "God, we need more preachers. . . . I said that right—we need more preachers because they know how to create community."

Putnam also warned, "From a civic point of view, a new Great Awakening (if it happened) would not be an unmixed blessing. . . . Proselytizing religions are better at creating bonding social capital than bridging social capital, and tolerance of unbelievers is not a virtue notably associated with fundamentalism."[10]

This warning against the possible bad effects of religious revivals is important. Yet the kind of social capital for which Putnam is calling is precisely what Wesleyans do when we start new congregations or new small groups in our churches. The kind of strong bonding social capital that is also strong in bridging cultural differences is precisely what the future Wesleyan movement must embrace.

Moisés Naím's analysis in *The End of Power* is captured in the long subtitle of his book: *From Boardrooms to Battlefields and Churches to States, Why Being in Charge Isn't What It Used to Be.* He begins with the definition that power is "the capacity to get others to do, or to stop doing, something." Claiming it is undergoing "a historic and world-changing transformation," he continues, "Power is spreading and long-established, big players are increasingly being challenged by newer and smaller ones. And those who have power are more constrained in the ways they can use it."[11]

Naím claims that there have been three revolutions that have opened up possibilities for agile, smaller, and newer groups to challenge the dominance enjoyed by larger entities. On the battlefield, consider how the United States Army has been challenged by Al Qaeda and ISIS. Think how Apple challenged IBM. Think about how Pentecostals challenged the Roman Catholic Church in Latin America.

Naím summarizes the change by naming three revolutions. The first is the "more" revolution. He writes,

> Ours is an age of profusion. There is simply more of everything now. There are more people, countries, cities, political

parties, armies; more goods and services, and more companies selling them; more weapons and more medicines; more students and more computers; more preachers and more criminals. The world's economic output has increased fivefold since 1950. Income per capita is three and a half times greater than it was then. More importantly, there are more people—2 billion more than there were just two decades ago.[12]

His conclusion is that "when people are more numerous and living fuller lives, they become more difficult to regiment and control."[13] This "more" revolution was accompanied by the mobility revolution. There are more than 214 million migrants throughout the world. Urbanization is a global phenomenon that means more people are leaving rural areas and settling in large cities. The movement of money and goods and services as well as people means that old patterns are dying out and new opportunities for influence and leadership present themselves. In such a highly mobile world, life is easier for challengers and harder for traditional leaders.[14]

Naím's third revolution is the mentality revolution. Here he argues that there has been a profound change in "expectations and standards" so that "most people look at the world, their neighbors, employers, clergy, politicians and governments with different eyes than their parents did."[15] This change in mentality is fueled by the Internet and television as well as by the more and mobility revolutions. His argument could be supplemented by chronicling the level of trust expressed by the baby-boomer generation for all kinds of authorities: political, religious, corporate, and educational.

Many of Naím's proposed solutions are aimed at political life in various countries. Two of his suggestions apply to the church as well. He strongly recommends that leaders work hard to rebuild trust between leaders and the people and work hard to increase participation. His remedies are similar to those of Thomas Friedman in *The World Is Flat* in which Friedman argues that collaboration is the key to both big and small companies succeeding in a world driven by connectivity.[16]

Taken together, Naím and Friedman are describing a world in which the patterns that shaped much of Western culture in 1950 are now radically different. It is easy to point out the changes in technology and communication, but Naím is showing how many different patterns have converged to make the world a radically different place than it used to be.

Whereas the Wesleyan movement was much more influential in the world in 1950 than it is today, some of the reasons for our decline is related to the three revolutions he has described. People have more religious options than ever before. We are in a context in which there is much greater competition for the hearts and minds of people.

Kenda Creasy Dean has also described a different kind of cultural change that affects the future of the Wesleyan movement. Her *Almost Christian: What the Faith of Our Teenagers Is Telling the American Church* interprets data from the 2003–2005 National Study of Youth and Religion. This survey focused on adolescent spirituality in the United States. Her opening chapter states the primary thesis cogently:

> The problem does not seem to be that churches are teaching young people badly, but that we are doing an exceedingly

good job of teaching youth what we really believe: namely that Christianity is not a big deal, that God requires little, and that the church is a helpful social institution filled with nice people focused primarily on "folks like us"—which, of course, begs the question of whether we are really the church at all.[17]

She cites the authors of the national study, who conclude, "Moralistic Therapeutic Deism is, in the context of [teenagers'] own congregations and denominations, actively displacing the substantive traditional faiths of conservative, black, and mainline Protestantism, Catholicism, and Judaism in the United States."[18]

On their view, the characteristics of moralistic therapeutic deism start with the affirmation that there is a God. This God is described by most religions as desiring persons to be good, nice, and fair. God's desire is that people be happy and feel good about themselves. However, God is not involved in one's life unless they ask for help. On the other hand, people who are good to go heaven when they die.[19]

One of the key messages of Dean's argument is that Christianity has so weakened its message that younger generations regard it is not worth believing. However, she does note that 8 percent of American youth can be classified as highly devoted. They make use of four cultural tools: "(1) they confess their tradition's *creed*, of God-story; (2) they belong to a *community* that enacts the God-story; (3) they feel *called* by this story to contribute to a larger purpose; and (4) they have *hope* for the future promised by this story."[20]

Taken as a whole, the description of the context for Christianity in America at the start of the twenty-first century is sobering. Following Jesus as a Wesleyan is not as easy today as it was in the 1950s. Yet each of these analysts offers ideas about how religious people might address the challenges we face and contribute to what is really needed. Putnam explicitly calls for a new great awakening with the kind of balance between religious conviction and tolerance for which Methodists are known. Naím suggests that rebuilding trust between leaders and people is crucial along with increasing opportunities for participation in decision-making processes. Dean identifies the theological weaknesses of Christianity and suggests that a refocus on the gospel and its lived practices is the way forward.

How Do United Methodists Feel about Our Recent Past?

A number of years ago my brother, Greg Jones, was riding on a plane and engaged the person sitting next to him in conversation. It turns out he was a consultant working with nonprofit organizations and had been involved with The United Methodist Church during the conversations about the Call to Action. Finding out that Greg was a leader in the church, he made a comment and then asked a question: "I think The United Methodist Church is a wonderful church. You all do some amazing things all over the world. What puzzles me is why you are so down on yourselves. When are you going to quit bad-mouthing your own denomination?"

This uneasiness with our situation began to manifest itself in the 1980s. A number of people began to call attention to the persistent membership losses and worship attendance decline that had begun in the 1960s. A turning point came in 1986 when Bishop Richard Wilke wrote *And Are We Yet Alive? The Future of The United Methodist Church.* Elected as a bishop in 1984, he dedicated the book "To the Church I love and serve." The opening sentence was a sea change from what other bishops and church leaders had been saying. He wrote, "Our sickness is more serious than we at first suspected. We are in trouble, you and I, and our United Methodist Church. We thought we were just drifting, like a sailboat on a dreamy day. Instead, we are wasting away like a leukemia victim when the blood transfusions no long work."[21]

Wilke then reviewed the facts and called for better leadership, a clearer focus on our mission, and a renewed commitment to evangelism in a changed world. For me as a young pastor serving his first full-time appointment in a local church, his book was a breakthrough. At last a leader was telling the truth and offering a clear way forward.

Another turning point for our church came in 1996 when the General Conference approved a new mission statement. Two crucial sentences were added to the *Book of Discipline*: "The mission of the Church is to make disciples of Jesus Christ. Local churches provide the most significant arena through which disciple-making occurs."[22] (In 2008 the words "for the transformation of the world" were added at the end of the first sentence). This change launched a twenty-year discussion about what it means to "make disciples" and how clarity about our mission can and should help align our resources for that purpose. Bishops, general agencies, and annual conferences have worked hard at the four focus areas. They are currently described as the following:

1. Engaging in ministry with the poor

2. Improving global health

3. Developing principled Christian leaders

4. Creating new and renewed congregations

Many conferences have worked hard at starting new congregations and revitalizing existing ones. The journey of changing old ways of being church and finding new patterns of missional effectiveness has been difficult.

Perhaps the best metaphor for the last forty years of The United Methodist Church was coined by Gil Rendle in his *Journey in the Wilderness: New Life for Mainline Churches.* He wrote, "It isn't that often that a whole people go through a religious wilderness together. Yet in North America that has been the case in my lifetime and in my experience." He continues to describe the wilderness in positive terms:

I am encouraged. The longer I am in this wilderness, the greater my hope grows. For I have been witness to people all around me who have been open to learning new ways to live what were earlier and deeply established identities. Above all else the wilderness is a place to learn. The wilderness is where we learn again to live in a new way because old supports are gone, old assumptions no longer hold true, and old practices either fail or are no longer possible. To live, the people must learn anew even the most basic things that in the old homeland were hidden by our easy assumptions and learned behavior.[23]

Rendle's reframing of the situation being faced by mainline churches is extraordinarily helpful. I fully believe that most United Methodist congregations are fully ready to be missionally effective if the 1950s ever come back. The fact that it is no longer the 1950s and that they are not coming back means that we are disoriented and uneasy. Rendle and others have called to mind the journey from Egypt to the promised land and have noted that such a journey is a time of preparing for a new reality. We have learned a lot during the last fifty years. I have a sense that we should harvest what we have learned and apply it more directly than we have to date.

What is required from us now is a both/and approach to our situation. At our best we are not hiding from the facts. We are focused on the negative trends we have been experiencing, and we are facing reality. At the same time, we are also focusing on the incredible resources we still have and the amazing signs of vitality we experience all around us. We have been learning and we are finding our way forward. We are aware of the dangers and the opportunities of our current situation.

What Should We Teach?
How Shall We Teach?
What Shall We Do?

Harvesting what we have learned in the wilderness and applying it means it is time for action. It is helpful to formulate that course of action by referring to the three basic questions Wesleyans ask themselves when they gather to discern God's leading of their movement. In 1744, at the first conference of Methodist preachers, the agenda had three questions:

1. What to teach

2. How to teach, and

3. What to do (that is, how to regulate our doctrine, discipline, and practice)[24]

Given the description of our missional context and the resources we can gather from our past, I believe there are ten characteristics that will define a vibrant Wesleyan movement in the future. Such a movement will

- preach and maintain Wesleyan doctrine

- invite persons to live the Wesleyan way of salvation

- preach personal holiness

- preach and live social justice

- focus on the Holy Spirit

- be flexible in structure

- empower laity for mission, including evangelism
- emphasize the means of grace
- form spiritual communities, especially in families
- be united in diversity

The following chapter will explain each of these in more detail under the headings of doctrine, spirit, and discipline.

Doctrine, Spirit, and Discipline

How is it possible that United Methodism, a movement that spread scriptural holiness across America and throughout the world, is now in decline and has turned toward maintenance rather than mission? John Wesley was struggling with a similar question in 1786 when he published these words in the *Arminian Magazine* under the title "Thoughts upon Methodism":

> I am not afraid that the people called Methodists should ever cease to exist either in Europe or America. But I am afraid lest they should only exist as a dead sect, having the form of religion without the power. And this undoubtedly will be the case unless they hold fast both the doctrine, spirit, and discipline with which they first set out....
>
> How then is it possible that Methodism, that is, the religion of the heart, though it flourishes now as a green bay-tree, should continue in this state? For the Methodists in every

place grow diligent and frugal; consequently they increase in goods. Hence they proportionably increase in pride, in anger, in the desire of the flesh, the desire of the eyes, and the pride of life. So, although the form of religion remains, the spirit is swiftly vanishing away.

Is there no way to prevent this? This continual declension of pure religion? . . . There is one way, and there is no other under heaven. If those who *gain all they can*, and *save all they can*, will likewise *give all they can*, then the the more they will grow in grace, and the more treasure they will lay up in heaven.[1]

For Wesley the diagnosis was about the accumulation of riches and the spiritual dangers posed by the attraction of things. While Wesley may be right, in this essay I have offered a more complicated analysis of how United Methodism has declined. Consequently, the prescription I offer will be more complicated. Yet my prescriptions are best understood as simply a new approach to the three headings of "doctrine, spirit, and discipline," which Wesley mentioned long ago.

Doctrine

Preach and Maintain Wesleyan Doctrine

In the list of questions each bishop is supposed to ask persons before they are ordained elder are the following:

Have you studied the doctrines of The United Methodist Church?

After full examination do you believe that our doctrines are in harmony with the Holy Scriptures?

Will you preach and maintain them?[2]

Almost all candidates for ordination answer yes to all three. In my conference these questions are asked in front of the entire annual conference so that there are as many witnesses as possible to the important commitments being made in the ordination ritual.

But these questions raise two important prior questions that are not sufficiently understood. The first one is, "What are the doctrines of The United Methodist Church?" In an earlier book I argued that the official doctrine of the UMC is constituted by ten texts in three levels of authority. The highest level is that of the constitutional standards of doctrine. These include the Constitution, the Articles of Religion, the Confession of Faith, John Wesley's Standard Sermons, his Explanatory Notes upon the New Testament, and the General Rules. The next lower level of authoritative documents are the contemporary statements of the General Conference. These are contained in the nonconstitutional sections of *The Book of Discipline* and *The Book of Resolutions*. The lowest level of authority is contained in liturgical documents—namely, *The United Methodist Hymnal* and *United Methodist Book of Worship*.[3]

The difficulty for United Methodists is putting all of these together in a workable whole that informs one's ministry and the congregation's activities. That is the point of the second question, "What does it mean to preach and maintain those doctrines?" I take this question to be focusing on the basic purpose and shape of one's entire ministry. In short, everything one says and does should aim at embodying the way of life described by the church's doctrine.

Thus, how one puts together these ten documents into a workable whole is absolutely crucial. It will shape the content of one's preaching, the priorities for one's use of time, and the way one lives. One important way that the denomination has summarized its doctrine is in the one-sentence opening of its mission statement: "The mission of the Church is to make disciples of Jesus Christ for the transformation of the world."[4] When the first formulation of this was adopted in 1996, it was intended to be a touchstone to guide all aspects of the church to align resources for missional purposes. More recently, the Council of Bishops and the Connectional Table have said in their Call to Action that the denomination's primary challenge is "to redirect the flow of attention, energy, and resources to an intense concentration on fostering and sustaining an increase in the number of vital congregations effective in making disciples of Jesus Christ for the transformation of the world."[5] Vital congregations are those that preach Wesleyan doctrine and then have ministries that serve as channels of God's grace to help persons make progress along the way of salvation.

Invite Persons to Live the Wesleyan Way of Salvation

The phrase "make disciples of Jesus Christ for the transformation of the world" is another way of expressing the mission that was true of the earliest Wesleyan movement. In the first American discipline after the Christmas Conference, the question was written, "Q. What may we reasonably believe to be God's Design in raising up the Preachers called *Methodists?* A. To reform the Continent, and to spread scriptural Holiness over these Lands."[6] By "scriptural holiness" the eighteenth-century Methodists meant the way of life contained in the Bible. Wesley believed the way of salvation to be the main subject of scripture, what he called its "general tenor." Wesley formulated these steps in different ways at different times, but his views can be summarized as the following:

- Creation in the image of God

- Original sin

- Repentance

- Justification by faith

- Sanctification by faith

- Perfection

Wesley frequently emphasized that we are saved by grace through faith for good works, as pithily taught in Ephesians 2:8-10. Thus, for each of these stages it is appropriate to talk about how the grace of God is leading the individual to make progress toward the ultimate goal of entire sanctification. In one place, he summarized God's work as "preventing, justifying or sanctifying grace."[7]

Thus, when the UMC describes its mission as "making disciples of Jesus Christ for the transformation of the world," it is proclaiming its role as a means of God's grace. It affirms that all persons are valuable in God's sight as creatures created in God's own image. It also affirms that every human being is a sinner in need of God's forgiveness and transforming power. The church then teaches that every person needs to repent, which means to turn his or her life Godward. Justification is the decision point where one decides to accept God's offer of salvation and to become a disciple of Jesus. It is the identity point where one moves from being a seeker to a self-avowed Jesus-follower. Justification is normally accompanied by baptism (if not experienced previously) and church membership. The rest of one's life is sanctification—growing by grace through faith to become a mature Christian. Such maturity involves giving one's time, talents, and money to be used by God to transform the world.

Transformation of the world is multifaceted. Part of it means bringing the world to worship the one true God and God's only Son, Jesus Christ. The hymn in Philippians 2 is still our prayer, that

> at the name of Jesus everyone
> > in heaven, on earth, and under the earth might bow
> and every tongue confess that
> > Jesus Christ is Lord, to the glory of God the Father
> > (Phil 2:10-11)

Such transformation should not be superficial, but to have all human beings become fully devoted followers of Jesus.

On our understanding as Wesleyans, such devotion means our hearts will be transformed and the world filled with love of God and love of neighbor. Hence the next two characteristics of the Wesleyan movement.

Preach Personal Holiness

In Wesley's "The Character of a Methodist," he emphasizes that a Methodist is someone who has "the love of God shed abroad in his heart by the Holy Ghost given unto him"; one who "loves the Lord his God with all his heart, and with all his soul, and with all his mind, and with all his strength" and who "accordingly loves his neighbour as himself; he loves every man as his own soul." Wesley continues,

> And the tree is known by its fruits. For as he loves God, "so he keeps his commandments." Not only some, or most of them, but all, from the least to the greatest. He is not content to "keep the whole law, and offend in one point," but has, in all points, "a conscience void of offence towards God and towards man." Whatever God has forbidden he avoids; whatever God hath enjoined, he doth—and that whether it be little or great, hard or easy, joyous or grievous to the flesh. He "runs the way of God's commandments, now he hath set his heart at liberty." It is his glory, I say, so to do; it is his daily crown of rejoicing, to "do the will" of God "on earth, as it is done in heaven"; knowing it is the highest privilege of "the angels of God, of those that excel in strength, to fulfil his commandments, and hearken to the voice of his word."[8]

The Wesleyan vision of personal holiness takes all God's commandments seriously. Wesley's series of sermons on the Sermon on the Mount is the most visible place where he works out what it means to love God and to love one's neighbor with all of one's being.

We live in a time when the cultural consensus about personal morality has collapsed. Far too often for Christians the city, state, and national laws are seen as the way in which morality is decided. Yet the civil and criminal laws should be seen as the lowest common denominator of what is moral and ethical in society. Honesty, integrity, compassion, concern for the environment, generosity, and other character traits are crucial for the Christian life. The New Testament, taken as a whole, provides a number of measures for how Christians are doing in their journey toward entire sanctification. The parable of the sheep and the goats in Matthew 25 sets a high standard of care for those in need. Galatians 5:22-23 describes the fruit of the Spirit as love, joy, peace, patience, kindness, generosity, faithfulness, gentleness, and self-control.

At the same time, a variety of behaviors are condemned and prohibited for Christians. Galatians 5:19-21 describes them as selfish desires ("works of the flesh" in King James idiom) and lists "sexual immorality, moral corruption, doing whatever feels good, idolatry, drug use and casting spells, hate, fighting, obsession, losing your temper, competitive opposition, conflict, selfishness, group rivalry, jealousy, drunkenness, partying, and other things like that." Matthew 25 makes it clear that ignoring the hungry and failing to welcome the stranger are prohibited behaviors.

The magnificent future of the Wesleyan movement means that we must be forthright in naming the contours of personal holiness. In the current political climate, an emphasis on truthfulness, honesty, compassion, mutual respect, and civility is important. Developing a clear set of teachings on sexual morality is an important issue for any culture. Whereas same-gender marriage gets significant attention, both pro and con, it is actually the prevalence of divorce and unformed families that is causing greater harm.

Wesley frequently quoted the passage from Hebrews 12:14: "Pursue the goal of peace along with everyone—and holiness as well, because no one will see the Lord without it." The goal of the Christian life is that kind of holiness, which God wants for God's people individually and collectively.

Preach and Live Social Justice

The Wesleyan vision of holiness progressed to the extent that modern, Western culture progressed. In some respects, Christians have always articulated a desire for social justice, relying on the prophets' critiques of immoral social practices in ancient Israel. Wesleyan views of social justice have their roots in our eighteenth-century witness against slavery and the use of distilled liquor. Over time Wesleyans came to argue against the use of all forms of alcohol, advocating total abstinence. We also developed a witness against the use of tobacco, and many Wesleyans were advocates for women's rights. All of these socially just advocacy positions arose because Wesleyans saw the larger harm done to individuals by practices supported by the larger society.

Two factors enhanced the development of a social justice perspective for Christians. First, the developing academic disciplines of social work and sociology brought critical thinking to bear on long-standing problems such as domestic violence, abuse, and drunkenness. People began to formulate different approaches to thinking about such problems from systemic perspectives. As industrialization and urbanization increased in the late nineteenth century, Christians began to realize that poverty was sometimes caused by large social trends and not simply by individual behavior. A key turning point was the adoption of the Social Principles by the Methodist Episcopal Church in 1908. Ever since then Methodist and United Methodist churches have had official statements about principles to address holiness issues from a societal perspective.

Second, the success of the movements to end slavery, to provide for women's rights, and to combat alcoholism indicated that focused efforts on bringing change to a society can often have positive effects. Christians who care about holiness can achieve their goals through political action and efforts at social change.

Social holiness has both personal and advocacy perspectives. From the personal perspective, one ought to discipline one's life to support the social justice perspectives that Christians ought to follow. If we are opposed to racism, we should live in such a way as to embrace persons of different ethnicities.

We should give our time to events and organizations that enhance racial reconciliation. We should resist the institutional and societal patterns that make racism appear to be normal or acceptable.

The same applies for other issues as well. Concern for the environment would lead us to minimize energy usage and maximize recycling efforts. Concern for women's rights would move beyond simply accepting women's leadership to helping raise up a new generation of female leaders. Concern for the poor would lead one to participate in antipoverty efforts with one's time, talents, and money.

But social justice also involves advocacy for change in communities, organizations, and our nation. The classic example of this in my lifetime was the civil rights movement of the 1950s and 1960s, when some Christian leaders advocated for congressional legislation guaranteeing the right to vote and ending legal segregation according to race. Since that time, many movements have addressed many different social justice issues, seeking to help our cities, our states, our nations, and our world address problems as varied as global warming and human trafficking.

Within the Wesleyan movement, there is a broad consensus that social justice is part of the holiness "because no one will see the Lord without it" (Heb 12:14). However, there is controversy on two different aspects of this part of the Christian life. First, there is rarely agreement about which injustice is most important to address. Different social problems have their advocates, and there is often stiff competition for the attention of individual Christians, congregations, and the church as a whole. If ten persons each made a list of the ten most important social justice issues needing our attention, there is a high probability that there would be little agreement about which issues should be on the list and how they should be ranked.

Second, for any given problem, there are often varying diagnoses of its cause and the appropriate solution. This has led to great conflict among Wesleyans about what social justice should look like. During the Iraq War, I was asked by a news reporter, "How can George W. Bush [then president of the United States] be a Christian?" I answered, "You should realize that both George W. Bush and Hilary Rodham Clinton are active, faithful United Methodists who believe God has called them to make the world a better place. They both think they are serving the Lord in their political work. They simply disagree about what needs to be done and how to do it." United Methodists discuss these matters in our conferences where we seek to bring a variety of Christian perspectives to bear. But the more complex the issue, the more it is likely that faithful, reasonable Christians will disagree.

It is crucial that Wesleyans continue to address social issues in part because observers inside and outside the church wonder if the Christian faith matters. When we address issues such as homelessness, racism, sexism, immigration reform, and global warming it demonstrates that the love of God and God's passion for justice are embodied in our community. We should recognize that a movement as large and diverse as ours will have many different persons working hard at their particular issues, and we can be grateful that so many are working so hard in so widely different areas.

Spirit

Focus on the Holy Spirit

One of my publicly acknowledged sins is that of works righteousness. I tend to think that God's work is all up to me and that I should count on my own abilities, colleagues, and resources to accomplish any particular task. I behave all too often as if there was no Holy Spirit at work guiding the church. While I confess this sin daily, my improvements in trusting the spirit and providing room for the Spirit to be at work have made far too little progress.

Among United Methodists, I may not be alone. And I do draw comfort from Philippians 2:12-13: "Therefore, my loved ones, just as you always obey me, not just when I am present but now even more while I am away, carry out your own salvation with fear and trembling. God is the one who enables you both to want and to actually live out his good purposes."

I believe that the renewal of God's church is the work of the Holy Spirit and that a spiritual revival is at the heart of any plan for the future of the Wesleyan movement. There are leaders in the church who are more Spirit-led than I am, so I am going to discuss this aspect of our movement in a highly personal way, knowing that I need to focus on the Spirit's role in leading the church and that these may be more my personal agenda than something we all need to think about. At my best, making room for the Spirit to work involves at least four activities on my part: prayer, openness, attentiveness, and risk-taking.

First, I need to pray. I have been praying daily for the renewal and faithfulness of The United Methodist Church. I have prayed for specific pastors and congregations, for conferences and groups. I need to pray more about where God would lead me to apply my time and energy. The writing of this book was one such answer to prayer, as I began to ask God how I can contribute to the conversation about our future as Wesleyan Christians. More time listening for God's direction may make me more available to effective service for God's mission.

Second, I need to be open. Too often I have an idea and I am working on the strategic plan for its execution. I have gifts in administration and I can clearly see my way to get from our present situation to the preferred future. Unfortunately, my focus on the plan sometimes keeps me from seeing other possibilities that I had not previously considered. I should remember that many others are seeking to give the same faithful service to Christ that I would offer, and many of them may have found better ways of reaching our common goal. Openness is one aspect of my awareness to which I do not have all the answers, and to which others may have ideas or perspectives that will help the church be more missionally effective.

Third, I need to be attentive to other efforts and developments in light of God's amazing activities to accomplish God's purposes. This is a very chaotic time in American religious culture, and there are many different experiments being undertaken in a wide variety of settings. I must give the time to attend to how God is working in those other places so that I can learn from them what might work in my own context. When my attention is narrowly focused on the task I have set for myself, I may be oblivious to the work of the Spirit in another place. Attentiveness is the proactive side of openness; if I am open, then I need to give attention to those places where the Spirit might be at work.

Fourth, I need to take risks and try new possibilities. There have been times in my life when I thought the Spirit was leading me, but I lacked certainty. The path ahead was unclear, and there were significant risks of failure, damage to others, or both. On some of those occasions, the risky steps I took did in fact fail. But they allowed me to fail forward and to try something else that ended up succeeding. On other occasions, however, my willingness to follow an unknown path has been very successful, and I credit the leading of Holy Spirit for that success. If I had been too cautious, nothing would have happened. Focusing on the Spirit means sometimes getting out of one's comfort zone and taking a risk.

Be Flexible in Structure

Comparing the length and complexity of the *Book of Discipline* from 2012 with any of its predecessors from the nineteenth century gives a stark awareness of how our church has changed in the last 150 years. When Methodism was growing, the *Book of Discipline* was normally found in Methodist households along with the Bible. It was then called *The Doctrines and*

Discipline of the Methodist Episcopal Church. Over the years, General Conference has seen fit to add more and more regulations governing everything from committee membership in local churches to limitations on the power of bishops. For the first 150 years following the Christmas Conference, the church functioned as a two-pole structure—bishops and the conferences. In 1939 the Judicial Council was added to adjudicate episcopal interpretations of the church's laws. As the number of rules multiplied, the Judicial Council's interpretations built up a body of case law that also must be taken into account. Bishops, conference committees, and others responsible for the administration of the church sometimes find themselves wondering if new initiatives can withstand a Judicial Council challenge.

Then there is the question of whether any parts of the *Book of Discipline* can be adapted by a Central Conference for the special circumstances outside the United States. In 2012 the General Conference clarified that the Constitution, doctrinal statements, Ministry of All Christians, and Social Principles are not adaptable.[9] Whether any or all of Part VI, "Organization and Administration," is adaptable is the question.

Currently, the Standing Committee on Central Conference Matters is leading a study that may result in action at the 2020 General Conference. Rather than exporting overregulation to regions that have yet to completely follow all of the rules (even though they are supposed to do so), it would be better if the General Conference simplified the structure to provide greater flexibility everywhere. We need to increase our flexibility to adapt to changing missional contexts. This will require placing greater trust in our leaders, which will in turn require greater accountability from those trusted leaders.

Empower Laity for Mission, Including Evangelism

When the Wesleyan movement was growing, it was led by laity. It is time for laity to take the lead again. During the 1989–90 conference year, Bishop Bruce Blake made presentations to the people of the North Texas Conference under the title "Every United Methodist an Evangelist." He urged every lay person, along with the clergy, to undertake the role of sharing the good news of Christ and inviting the unchurched to become practicing Christians. Many United Methodist congregations will list on their leadership page a line such as "Ministers: Every member." In 1987 John Ed Mathison published *Every Member in Ministry*. In it he described the system used at Frazer Memorial United Methodist Church to get laity involved in meaningful ministry.

This trend of empowering laity will build upon important trends among younger people in America. It is often remarked that persons want to use their gifts and talents to make a difference rather than serving on a committee that makes decisions. A number of churches are using spiritual gifts inventories or are seeking to have people self-identified where they can best make a contribution of their time and talents.

In my "20 Components of an Evangelistically Effective Congregation," the sixth component is "Empower Laity to

Witness Verbally to Their Friends, Associates, Relatives, and Neighbors." It is described as follows:

> a. All laypersons should understand themselves to be verbal witnesses for Christ (1 Peter 3:15-16). They are in contact with pre-Christian and unchurched persons and they are more effective witnesses than clergy.
>
> b. This witness can simply be talking about their church or inviting unchurched friends to come.
>
> c. Programs such as Bring a Friend Sunday, Home for Christmas, Faith-Sharing and Witness may be helpful in giving laity confidence in verbal witness.
>
> d. Three different types of faith-sharing are inviting, telling, and mentoring. All Christians can invite, some are able and should be encouraged to tell, and a few should be trained as mentors.[10]

The future Wesleyan movement should raise expectations of what the Christian life involves. For many years, pastors invited persons to church membership. Membership became equivalent to joining any civic organization where there were dues, occasional attendance at meetings, and occasional volunteer opportunities. In the future Wesleyans should be inviting persons to discipleship where all of one's heart, soul, and mind is offered to the love of God and neighbor. This includes one's time, talents, and finances.

The future Wesleyan movement will need genuine disciples who are carrying the gospel in word and deed to a world that is increasingly hostile and complex.

Discipline

Emphasize the Means of Grace

Protestant Christians, including United Methodists and other Wesleyans, all too often have a weak doctrine of the church. Roman Catholics and Orthodox Christians tend to have a higher ecclesiology. In practical terms this may be expressed by the views of believers about whether it is necessary or even important to belong to a congregation.

It is frequently heard from people, "I am a Christian, but I just don't belong to a church." Or "I'm spiritual but not religious." It is also the case that most Protestant congregations have a lot of inactive members who never attend worship and never participate in the church's ministries. They believe that having their name on the membership roll is sufficient identification as a disciple of Christ.

The future Wesleyan movement will teach clearly that being a Christian means active participation in a gathered community of believers. John Wesley understood that the New Testament knows nothing of solitary Christianity. He wrote,

> First, I shall endeavour to show, that Christianity is essentially a social religion, and that to turn it into a solitary religion is indeed to destroy it.

By Christianity I mean that method of worshipping God which is here revealed to man by Jesus Christ. When I say this is essentially a social religion, I mean not only that it cannot subsist so well, but that it cannot subsist at all without society, without living and conversing with other men.[11]

In the eighteenth-century Wesleyan movement, to be a Methodist meant one belonged to a class meeting and was regular in attendance. If one was not practicing this means of grace, one was expelled from the Methodist society by simply not having one's ticket renewed the next quarter.

The theological rationale for this is that believers are baptized into Christ. The church is the body of Christ and thus, when one is baptized, one is always incorporated into a particular congregation. God has promised that where two or three are gathered in Christ's name, there Christ will be present. It is in the church that the grace of Christ is reliably present. While God's grace can in fact be experienced in additional places and through additional means, Wesley taught that the ordinary channels for saving grace are those found in the church. It is appropriate for Wesleyans to understand that the church itself is a means of grace.

How this gets lived out is an important consideration. One congregation had an approach called "worship plus two," with the number referring to small groups. Before joining the church as members, they were told that membership had no privileges. In fact, a new member lost the privilege of parking in the visitors' parking spaces. Instead, joining was a step forward in the discipleship journey that would help them grow toward Christian maturity. Membership brought additional expectations for which the congregation and its staff would hold them accountable. Members were expected to worship weekly either at that church or at another one if they were travelling. Members were expected to belong to a small group from which they were spiritually fed. They were expected to belong to another small group in which they served others. They were expected to tithe or move toward tithing. In light of the evangelistic task, I would add to the list the expectation that each person invite at least one unchurched friend to worship each year.

Over the last several decades The United Methodist Church, along with other denominations, has reduced the expectations placed on its members. Many observers have described current religious trends as a consumer culture in which persons participate in church as if they were consumers of religious activities performed by clergy and other paid staff. Rather than asking how they can offer themselves as part of God's saving activities in the world, church members have been asking how the church can meet their needs and desires. Such a consumer culture militates against genuine discipleship and the vitality of the church.

Form Spiritual Communities, Especially in Families

In a time when social capital (as Putnam calls it) has been in decline for decades, one of the most important strategies for the church is to form spiritual communities. There is a sense in which the entire Wesleyan movement is a community with all of its diversity and geographic spread. There is another sense in which each congregation is such a community in which persons know one another and worship and serve with one another.

The first task of a vibrant Wesleyan movement is to form new congregations to reach new persons. Many United Methodist conferences have learned quite a bit about how best to form such congregations and have dedicated significant resources to doing so. There was a time in America during which laity took the lead in forming new congregations and then asked for a circuit rider to come and preach to them. In other situations, the preacher would announce the formation of a new congregation and gather the people together, organizing them into a community. Now congregations are so complex it is best if one is started by a conference.

The twenty-first century has seen major demographic changes in America and around the world. At our best Wesleyans are very adaptable, looking for places where God is opening doors to the forming of new congregations. Sometimes that is in an area of growing population. In other places there is a changing of the ethnic makeup of neighborhoods or cities. In other places older families are replaced by younger ones whose worship and programming styles are different from what the church has been offering in the past. We must become even more adept at identifying such evangelistic opportunities and then devote sufficient personnel and financial resources to plant new congregations.

Within new and existing congregations, it is also crucial to form new small groups. For any church that follows the "worship plus two" model of discipleship, it is necessary to be continually forming new small groups both for spiritual nurture and for service. Bishop Richard Wills, in his *Waking to God's Dream: Spiritual Leadership and Church Renewal*, describes how one congregation was strengthened by expecting every member to belong to a Wesley Group.[12] Every Wesley Group had the same five purposes: prayer, study, accountability, fellowship, and service. He once noted that the ushers in his church were a Wesley Group who met for an hour before worship each Sunday, praying for the first-time visitors who would be coming that day.

Yet another level of spiritual-community formation will be a focus on a vibrant Wesleyan movement. One of the most significant crises in American culture today is the breakdown of the family unit. There are far too many divorces and far too many children being raised by single parents. One of the most important ways to care for at-risk children is to strengthen family ties and to provide for better environments to prevent adverse childhood experiences. The church in its ministry with the poor can find ways of strengthening the parenting skills of those with responsibility for young children. While there are governmental policies that might address these issues as well, the church's ministry of strengthening marital ties and family structures is an important part of our future community-formation ministry.

Be United in Diversity

An article in *U.S. New and World Report* in 2015 conveyed the conclusions of the United States Census Bureau. After noting that a majority of the children under the age of five were born in diverse racial ethnic households, it said,

> The minority population is expected to rise to 56 percent of the total population in 2060, compared with the 38 percent last year. When that happens, "no group will have a majority share of the total and the United States will become a 'plurality' [nation] of racial and ethnic groups," the U.S. Census states. The minority-majority trend reflected among 5-year-olds is the beginning of that shift.[13]

Part of the shift in ethnic population percentages comes from a higher level of immigration. A Brookings Institution article reported that in 2014, a total of 20 million persons, or 13 percent of the US population, were born in foreign countries. This is the highest percentage since 1920.[14]

Part of the basic character—the DNA of the early Christian movement—was the ability to unite diverse groups of people into one community. The first Pentecost recounted in Acts 2 was a harbinger of what God would do through the Christian movement. Galatians 3:25-29 says it clearly:

> But now that faith has come, we are no longer under a custodian.
>
> You are all God's children through faith in Christ Jesus. All of you who were baptized into Christ have clothed yourselves with Christ. There is neither Jew nor Greek; there is neither slave nor free; nor is there male and female, for you are all one in Christ Jesus. Now if you belong to Christ, then indeed you are Abraham's descendants, heirs according to the promise.

And yet, there were tensions within the Christian community as people of different language groups, different social classes, and different types of spiritual experience sought to live together in the service of Christ. First Corinthians offers many insights into how the diversity of the early Christian movement was handled, and the metaphor of unity with diversity was taught with the image of the body of Christ and its various parts.

The twenty-first-century Wesleyan movement has incredible diversity. The United Methodist Church is one of the few worldwide churches, if by *church* one means unity in doctrine, discipline, and mission. Granted, it does not have congregations in every country, but its presence with congregations and bishops on four of the continents means it has the right to describe itself as "worldwide."

The crucial question for the future of the Wesleyan movement is the question of unity. Paragraph 101 defines our unity in these terms: "The *Book of Discipline* reflects our Wesleyan way of serving Christ through doctrine and disciplined Christian life. We are a worldwide denomination united by doctrine, discipline, and mission through our connectional covenant."[15]

Recent actions by annual conferences in the United States have broken that unity. The question before The United Methodist Church today is how to envision a looser form of unity that still preserves some connection in mission while allowing for different expressions of the Wesleyan movement.

Discarded Baggage

So far we have described a new cultural location for the Wesleyan movement. We find ourselves in a flat world with greatly reduced privileges and new forms of communication. The intellectual and communal competition for communities of Jesus-followers is increasingly complex.

Below I list seven pieces of baggage weighing down United Methodists and hindering our renewal as a movement. For each bag I sketch a replacement. Think of the baggage as a steamer trunk in which the accumulated possessions of decades are carried with you, but transporting it requires a truck with a hoist. We need to replace the steamer trunk in each case with a backpack more suitable for rapid movement in a fast car.

The difficulty is that each backpack requires a high level of trust given to leaders who can make decisions rapidly. Leadership, when exercised at its best, focuses on the mission of the church and is able to make decisions that will help it increase its fruitfulness. Rather than being mired in bureaucratic rules, they need to be freed to lead. However, we have had a lot of experience with leaders who either did not perform well or engaged in misconduct. All leaders, whether bishops or committees, must also be held accountable and easily changed when they do not function fruitfully for the movement.

From Distractions to Missional Effectiveness

The story of Mary and Martha in Luke 10:38-42 provides a significant lesson for the Wesleyan movement today:

> While Jesus and his disciples were traveling, Jesus entered a village where a woman named Martha welcomed him as a guest. She had a sister named Mary, who sat at the Lord's feet and listened to his message. By contrast, Martha was preoccupied with getting everything ready for their meal. So Martha came to him and said, "Lord, don't you care that my sister has left me to prepare the table all by myself? Tell her to help me."
>
> The Lord answered, "Martha, Martha, you are worried and distracted by many things. One thing is necessary. Mary has chosen the better part. It won't be taken away from her."

Martha was entertaining the Messiah in her home, and she knew there were many tasks to be accomplished. She complained that her sister was not working on those tasks. Instead of offering her sympathy, Jesus advised that "one thing is necessary."

The United Methodist Church has, over the decades, developed a wide variety of different groups, committees, boards, agencies, and ministries. We have built many different facilities and established many different related organizations. It is not unusual for a mature institution to have generated many different committees, working groups, and ministries. Over time, a good idea takes on a life of its own and develops its own set of supporters and goals.

Such distractions consume time, energy, and money at all levels of the church. At the congregational level, it sometimes means that relational issues take precedence over missional issues. Missionally effective congregations know that they must prioritize disciple-making over all possible distractions. A common distraction is the care of facilities as an end rather than a means. On the one hand, I know of one church that cares so deeply about the beauty and decorations of the parlor that it could be used only rarely lest it be damaged. On the other hand, another church cared so much about its children's ministry that it allowed red-colored juices to be served at children's events, knowing that the carpet might be stained. The contrast is clear: one church cared about discipling children, whereas the other cared about having a beautiful room.

One way of pursuing reform is to pay attention to the agenda for meetings of leadership groups. Each meeting might have just three items to consider:

1. What is our mission?

2. How are we doing?

3. What are we doing that is not contributing to our mission and thus we can quit doing it?

Weak Council of Bishops to Leadership Team

The Council of Bishops was once told by a consultant working on the Call to Action process, "You are a group of leaders. You are not a leadership group." He accurately noted that we are not acting together in a cohesive manner in ways where a group decision would then command support of all the bishops. We are not accountable to each other, and after a Council meeting each individual bishop would feel free to act and speak as she or he chooses. He noted that bishops would privately tell him how they disagreed with what they had just voted for, but they voted for it anyway. He noted that most of our conversations in plenary consisted of talking at one another rather than listening to one another.

The church needs a leadership team. A crucial part of our polity assumes that the Council will function well in its responsibility to "plan for the general oversight and promotion of the temporal and spiritual interests of the entire Church and for carrying into effect the rules, regulations, and responsibilities prescribed and enjoined by the General Conference and in accord with the provisions set forth in this Plan of Union."[1] Recent Judicial Council decisions as well as the hopes and aspirations of the General Conference assume that the Council functions as a cohesive team of leaders. While it has occasionally been able to accomplish key tasks, three factors have prevented it from being all that it could be.

First, the Council is too large. All retired bishops are members of the Council. Thus, during the last quadrennium, there were 152 members, all of whom have the right to speak at Council meetings. Only the sixty-six active bishops are allowed to vote, but everything we know about the functioning of leadership teams says that voice is more important than voting. Further, a group of 152 has a hard time functioning as a team. As of July 2016 we have now added fifteen new bishops to the group.

The best hope for the Council to become the leadership team that the church needs is to restrict its membership to only active bishops. When a bishop retires, he or she should retain the title and have a place of honor in the church. There are many ways in which retired bishops are functioning for the good of the church. Some are bishops in residence at colleges and seminaries. Some function as consultants for annual conferences. Some preside over church trials. But they should not attend the Council meetings where the active bishops are seeking to discern how to provide for the temporal and spiritual interests of the church.

One of the distractions is that the Council of Bishops has seen itself as a family and the relationships formed are strong and deep. Retired bishops like to attend Council meetings to see their colleagues and to stay in touch with what is happening in the life of the church. Thus, our care for them as retired and honored senior leaders has been more important than the leadership function of the Council. The church needs to find appropriate ways to care for our retired leaders while not impeding the Council's function as the executive branch of the denomination.

Second, the Council has been understaffed. For eight of the last twelve years it has had one full-time administrative assistant. Then four years ago it inherited the New York City–based staff of the former Commission on Christian Unity and Interreligious Concerns. Whenever the Council has undertaken significant initiatives, it has borrowed the services of general agency staff. While this has worked well in a number of situations, it is also the case that staff loyalty is always to their agency. Since 1972, the dynamics of general church leadership have been that bishops have tended to see themselves as servants of the general agencies rather than the general agencies seeing themselves as following the leadership of the bishops.

A major change is underway on this matter. The Council of Bishops is reconfiguring its staffing to provide much greater support for its ecumenical, faith and order and other activities. By locating all its staff in Washington, the Council is hoping to improve its ability to lead.

Third, bishops are not accountable to the Council, and thus they are able to act as they see fit. To the extent that bishops are held accountable at all, it is to the Jurisdictional or Central Conference and its Committee on Episcopacy. (Judicial Council decision 1230 rendered uncertain the process of the Jurisdictional Conference being able to hold a bishop accountable for his administration of the office.) In cases in which the Committee on Episcopacy has not functioned well, the Council has received requests to remedy the situation. In reality, the Council has no meaningful action it can take to hold a bishop accountable. There is a type of relational accountability in which bishops do listen to one another in the Council, but in cases of disagreement each bishop may pretty much act as he or she sees fit.

The Council of Bishops is making progress in becoming the leadership team the church needs it to be. The fourth recommendation of the Council's Call to Action, published in 2011, said,

> Reform the Council of Bishops, with the active bishops assuming (1) responsibility and public accountability for improving results in attendance, professions of faith, baptisms, participation in servant/mission ministries, benevolent giving, and lowering the average age of participants in local church life; and (2) establishing a new culture of accountability throughout the church.[2]

However, some of the legislative changes needed to continue the progress have been rejected by the last two General Conferences. Significant change is still needed.

Multiple General Agencies to Four Agencies

The 2012 and 2016 General Conferences grappled with the proposals for restructuring the general agencies of the church.

Each agency has important work to do and has its own constituency of supporters who believe that their particular work is a high priority for the denomination. Over forty-four years, however, each agency has gained considerable independence from the rest of the denomination. They have developed strong systems of influencing General Conference to write the legislation that will allow them to pursue their own agendas and to provide the funding for them to do it. There is no significant oversight by the whole Council of Bishops. Instead, any meaningful episcopal oversight comes from the individual bishops chosen to serve as the officers of that agency.

Attempts at coordination have been made ever since the current structure was put into place in 1972. However, the Judicial Council has struck down provisions for the General Council on Ministry and the Connectional Table to hold the agencies accountable to a coordinating body. Some decisions have said that such supervision rests with either the General Conference or the Council of Bishops. The end result has been that any collaboration between the agencies is voluntary on their part. It has not worked well.

The Call to Action document made its fifth recommendation in these words:

> Consolidate program and administrative agencies, align their work and resources with the priorities of the Church and the decade-long commitment to build vital congregations, and reconstitute them with much smaller competency-based boards of directors in order to overcome current lack of align-

ment, diffused and redundant activity, and higher than necessary expense due to independent structures.[3]

In my view, the various plans that were considered by the last two General Conferences did not go far enough to consolidate the General Agencies. There is a case for the independence and separation of three of them. The General Board of Pensions and Health Benefits receives no apportionment support and manages large amounts of money. It is perhaps the best run agency of the church. The Board of Publication, operating as The United Methodist Publishing House, is also a self-funded entity that is operating in a dynamic and rapidly changing marketplace. United Methodist Women is an entity that is also self-funding and should remain independent.

There is a weaker case that could be made for the independence of the General Council on Finance and Administration. It manages the Church's seven apportionment funds and also protects the connection's legal interests. Remaining independent could provide it with strong fiscal oversight for the rest of the agencies.

The rest of the agencies should be combined into one entity. The General Board of Church and Society, the General Board of Global Ministries, the General Board of Discipleship, the General Board of Higher Education and Ministry, the General Commission on United Methodist Men, the General Commission on the Status and Role of Women, the General Commission on Communication, the General Commission on Religion and Race, and the General Commission on Archives and History could all function better with one board of directors and a unified staff.

While this arrangement would save money, the greatest impact would be on improved alignment and collaboration. Programs such as Imagine No Malaria and New Places for New People would benefit if the agencies had unified staffing and budgets. Efforts at collaboration have improved over the last sixteen years, but working with nine separate agencies led by nine general secretaries with nine separate boards of directors makes the collaboration much more difficult than it should be.

Opaque Swollen Apportionments to Tithe Mission Share

Four key problems affect the apportionment system of funding connectional ministry in The United Methodist Church.

First, the current method of funding connectional ministry assumes that the national leadership knows best how much money local churches should contribute for each of the funds. This has led to a widespread perception that apportionments are a kind of tax. In some conferences, the apportionment burden has been applied most heavily to our largest and strongest congregations. In one instance I am aware of, the apportionments constituted 24 percent of the congregation's operating budget. If we are focused on increasing the number vital congregations, we need to leave more money in local churches and ask for less for connectional purposes.

Second, the system by which the General Council on Finance and Administration divides the budget among the US conferences includes an adjustment that puts more burden on states in which the economy is stronger than other states. This assumes that the United Methodist congregations in those states are also financially stronger because of their context. The formula that divides the apportionment burden among annual conferences is opaque and cannot be easily explained or justified. If one of our goals, given the context of American culture today, is to rebuild trust between leaders and the people, we need a transparent way of paying for connectional ministry.

Third, the overall apportionment burden will become unsustainable over time as our US membership continues to decline. Older members are more generous than are younger members, and at some point the overall giving to United Methodist causes will start to decline. Many of our congregations are experiencing a new reality. They are growing in worship attendance and membership but receiving less money. Such trends will only continue over time.

Fourth, every local church should be completely responsible for the pastoral compensation of its clergy. Some annual conferences continue to subsidize smaller churches by apportioning benefits on the conference level. For example, if clergy health insurance and pension contributions are apportioned, smaller churches with full-time clergy get help from the conference while larger, growing churches pay more than they should. If a church is able to pay for a full-time pastor, it should do so. If it has been in decline and needs to change to a less-than-full-time appointment, the decision to move to that level should not be hidden by conference subsidies. While many conferences have moved away from apportioning benefits, some are still masking the decline of small churches and hurting growing congregations.

An apportionment formula should function as a percentage of local church operating income. For example, local churches could be asked to contribute 2.5 percent of their operating income to the general church and 7.5 percent to their annual conference. Such a tithing formula would be easily explained and would share the connectional responsibility for funding equally according to financial capacity. Annual conferences would then work with their expected income to craft their conference budget, and the general church would make decisions about how to allocate its share among the various needs with which it deals. Over time if the local churches prosper, connectional funding will increase. If, however, decline continues, then the conferences and general church will be able to manage their activities in line with what the denomination can afford.

Bureaucratic Credentialing to Flexible Credentialing

The most important part of United Methodist polity is our clergy leadership deployment system. We need to find the best possible men and women who will preach the gospel and lead local churches to be vital mission stations for God's purposes.

The three most important factors in the renewal of the Wesleyan movement are leadership, leadership, and leadership. Even with all of the bureaucratic, cumbersome, and sometimes nonsensical structures we currently have, visionary leaders have achieved amazing success in many parts of The United Methodist Church. If all the baggage just discussed is replaced by the more flexible backpacks I described, the church will still not be renewed unless we find the right leadership to guide us.

There is no substitute for good judgment about leadership. Our bishops, cabinets, and boards of ordained ministry need to continually sharpen our ability to discern a person's gifts and graces and effectiveness in ministry. Greg Jones wrote in *Christian Social Innovation*, "We became preoccupied with questions of what and how without any awareness of the why. A contemporary commentator on our current plight might suggest that United Methodists are no longer organizing to beat the devil but rather organizing for the sake of organizing— a great definition of bureaucracy!"[4]

This description has too often been accurate for our bishops, boards of ordained ministry, and cabinets. Too often we believe that ordination is a right that should not be denied someone who has been in the process for a sufficient amount of time. I have watched persons get approved by various groups from local churches to cabinets because we lacked the nerve to say, "I am sorry, but I don't think you are called to the ministry."

The vibrant Wesleyan movement of the future will have flexible credentialing. In other words, it will be possible to ordain persons who have excellent gifts for ministry but may not have graduated from college. Boards of Ordained Ministry and cabinets will ask more questions about fruitfulness and few questions about checklists of steps completed.

Guaranteed Appointment to Missional Appointment

Our system of guaranteed appointment and the independence of boards of ordained ministry have arisen in reaction to the misuse of episcopal authority over time. We are now at a point where our systems have become too focused on protection of persons and not enough on fruitfulness. We need to end the perception that no bishop can lose his position for poor performance and that every pastor will get another appointment even if they have shown incompetence in the ministry.

Simply ending guaranteed appointment is not the best answer. Rather, a changed culture is needed among bishops, cabinets, and boards of ordained ministry that allows for quick and easy exit for persons who do not belong in the ministry. Too many cabinets and boards have functioned for too long as a protector of all clergy regardless of competence. Instead, when someone needs to find another career, they should be helped to do so.

The General Board of Pensions and several annual conferences have created transitional funds to help people leave ministry and start a new career. Such experiments should be expanded and strengthened.

The biggest change, however, lies with bishops. We need to use the authority vested in us to appoint people to places for missional reasons. Being distracted by a clergy career ladder, taking care of people we like, and protecting members of the club are all ways in which we bishops have not focused on the missional effectiveness of our churches. It is only bishops who can make the appointive process continually focus on this question: What appointments will maximize the missional effectiveness of all the churches in this conference? There will always be a shortage of the right persons to serve and a need for new persons to enter the ministry. But at any point in time the appointive system should seek the best possible answer to that key question.

Steamer Trunks to Backpacks

While writing this book I moved from the Great Plains Episcopal Area to the Houston Episcopal Area. Mary Lou and I are surrounded by boxes of our belongings. Some of them are precious and will be important to our future. We are going to need them to live our lives. However, I have too much stuff. My file boxes are too numerous. Even though I gave away more than fifty boxes of books, I still own volumes that I will never use again. Having moved, I can assure you that I am carrying with me baggage that could have been left behind or been given away.

The United Methodist Church has baggage that must be discarded if we are to become the more nimble, movemental institution God needs us to be. Whether I have identified the right baggage is highly debatable. But I hope this book contributes to a conversation about what can be discarded and what must be carried with us into our future as a Wesleyan movement.

A Future with Hope

Hope is not optimism. Hope is an attitude of trusting in God and God's promise to guide Christ's church into a better future. It can coexist with a realistic assessment of current reality. A key biblical text on hope is the word of Jeremiah to the exiles in Babylon: "I know the plans I have in mind for you, declares the LORD; they are plans for peace, not disaster, to give you a future filled with hope" (Jer 29:11). That message of hope came in the midst of their greatest despair. The temple had been destroyed, and they were living in exile in the land of a foreign god. They were not sure that they could worship the Lord of Israel in a foreign land. Yet, Jeremiah delivered God's word to them, promising them a future with hope.

Our hope for the future of God's church rests first and foremost on God. God has revived Christ's church before, and we trust that God will do it again. Part of the grounds for our hope is the knowledge of our past described in chapter 1. But it is also important to note the hopeful trends that are already showing up among committed Wesleyans in the United States. Such signs abound in many different places, but I would list five significant trends, which I see as a foretaste of good things to come to God's people.

New Generation of Young Leaders

My son Arthur Jones and I wrote a book together entitled *Ask: Faith Questions in a Skeptical Age.*[1] The book stimulates conversation about significant faith questions, such as the following:

- Can only one religion be true?

- Why is there suffering and evil?

- How can I believe in science and creation?

This study can be used by small groups, and we model the conversations that can be sparked in the group. For each of the eight sessions we filmed a group of five young clergy. They were literally in a restaurant gathered around a table. A box of interesting objects helped them focus their comments to one another. As I watched the filming and then viewed the finished DVD, I was deeply moved. Here were five intelligent, diverse young Christian leaders grappling with important issues. Each of them is a leader in her or his own setting, and I was encouraged.

Then a few months later I attended the New Room event sponsored by Seedbed. More than one thousand Wesleyans were gathered for worship and learning. The presentations, many of them by people under the age of thirty-five, were inspiring, and the preaching was tremendous. As I looked around the room, I realized that the five young women and men I had worked with on the *Ask* project were not alone; there were many more such young persons being called into ministry in the Wesleyan movement.

In the Great Plains Conference of The United Methodist Church, the median age of our clergy is fifty-seven. If retirement comes typically at age sixty-five, that means that one-half of our pastors will retire in the next eight years. Many church consultants and bishops notice that clergy are most effective in reaching persons who are within ten years of their own age, either older or younger. That means that our median-age clergy are quite effective in reaching people forty-seven to sixty-seven, and I suspect most United Methodist churches are doing well with that age group. In many different settings, I am meeting gifted young people who are offering themselves for both lay and clergy leadership in our church.

Adaptive Leadership

The time when persons could enter into United Methodist ministry hoping to spend a whole career maintaining what has already been built is gone. Now we need a leadership that can adapt the Wesleyan movement's historic purpose to a new missional context.

This adaptive leadership comes in two forms. First, we need lay and clergy leaders who can gain the trust of existing congregations and institutions and then cast a vision of new ways of making disciples of Jesus Christ for the transformation of the world. Old patterns must be protected and fruitful ministries must be respected, but now is the time to add new approaches. For example, when an urban neighborhood is changing creating a mission field with a different ethnic group, restarting a congregation as a second campus of a healthy church has often brought new vitality to an existing church. The key factor in successful transitions is the willingness of older members to welcome newcomers who are younger and more diverse than they have reached in the past.

For example, my wife, Mary Lou, and I participated in wonderful Sunday school classes for the last nineteen years. (Prior to that I was a pastor, and we associated with many different Sunday school classes). The classes at Trietsch Memorial UMC and First UMC of Wichita were sustaining and life-giving for us. They were composed of people who were similar to us in age and life circumstances. Churches should continue those kinds of groups because they are the backbone of the traditional congregation.

The task of adaptive leadership is to help our existing congregations see and embrace the missional opportunities around them. For example, surrounding many of our churches are young families having their first children. The parents' marriage is under stress, and many of them are facing uncertain financial times. What should our churches be doing to strengthen family life? Many other churches are surrounded by newcomers to our communities, some of whom are immigrants. What should our churches be doing to create spiritual communities for them? Many families in America are suffering from substance abuse, divorce, and out-of-wedlock childbirth. Some of our most vibrant churches are providing recovery worship services, divorce recovery groups, and support for single mothers to provide new forms of community and family for people going through difficult situations.

The second form of adaptive leadership is the opportunities presented by starting completely new ministries. This is the challenge posed in Greg Jones's *Christian Social Innovation*. There are new needs and unreached groups of people, so we need to encourage creative solutions to these problems and creative forms of congregations to reach these groups of people.

Throughout our denomination leaders are learning to think adaptively and are willing to take the risks associated with trying new things. The job of conference leaders, including bishops, is to create space to allow these adaptive leaders to flourish.

Focus on Congregations

For many years pastors came to believe that the purpose of their congregation was to serve the needs of the annual conference. Many of us spent years reshaping United Methodist culture to reverse that. The purpose of the annual conference is clear in ¶601 of the *Book of Discipline*: "The purpose of the annual conference is to make disciples of Jesus Christ for the transformation of the world by equipping its local churches for ministry and by providing a connection for ministry beyond the local church; all to the glory of God."[2]

Local churches are the most significant arena in which disciple-making occurs. While it also happens in extension ministries such as camps, hospitals, campus ministries, and social service agencies, it is upon the vitality of congregations that the strength of the Wesleyan movement rests.

One of the most hopeful signs was the Council of Bishops and Connectional Table adopting Call to Action. It named an adaptive challenge: "Thus, the adaptive challenge for The United Methodist Church is: To redirect the flow of attention, energy, and resources to an intense concentration on fostering and sustaining an increase in the number of vital congregations effective in making disciples of Jesus Christ for the transformation of the world."[3]

Since that time much more attention is being paid to strengthening our existing congregations and creating new, healthy congregations. We are learning how to measure vitality and are working to align resources to help achieve this crucial goal.

More and more, bishops and district superintendents are casting aside all of the accumulated distractions of the appointment-making process and focusing on how to appoint clergy who will help that particular congregation be the best that it can possibly be. While we remain committed to all of the factors that shape the ministry of clergy in our conferences, the priority is now on answering this question: "What assignment of clergy will maximize the missional effectiveness of all the local churches in this conference?" Many old patterns, such as seniority and a career ladder, have been minimized, and instead we are focusing on leadership to increase the fruitfulness of congregations.

Global Sharing

If by *global* one means a church with congregations on at least four continents, and if by *church* one means that it is a body united by its doctrine, discipline, and mission, then The United Methodist Church is one of very few truly global Christian churches in the world today.

Many will question this claim. But recent events have shown that the Anglican Communion is not a single church, because they do not share the same doctrine and discipline on church-dividing matters. Lutherans and Presbyterians are united by worldwide fellowships that are similar to the World Methodist Council, but again these are relational groups of different churches rather than a single church with organic unity.

When the United Methodist General Conference met in 2016, 360 of the 864 delegates (41 percent) were from outside the United States. They were voting on doctrine and church law that would be binding all over the world. It was amazing to watch the conversations and deliberations from such a widely diverse but unified group of people.

In an increasingly globalized world, it is a great advantage to have leaders from so many different countries sitting at the table and making decisions about key issues. The sharing that goes back and forth from one part of the world to the next strengthens each part. This positive global sharing comes in three ways.

First, there is a sharing of ideas. Some parts of our Wesleyan movement have greater clarity about how to serve Christ than does another part. Because we are united in one church with relationships of trust from working together, the opportunities for mutual enrichment are strong. For many years now the Great Plains Conference and one of its predecessors, the Kansas West Conference, have had a partnership with the Zimbabwe Episcopal Area. While people from Kansas supported mission projects in Zimbabwe, one of the key aspects of the partnership is Kansas learning from their African colleagues how to do evangelism. Leaders from Africa have toured Kansas, talking about how they start new churches and how they share their faith. A delegation from Kansas attended an event called an "Ebenezer," where fifty thousand persons worshipped, prayed, and learned in the national soccer stadium in Harare. At the same time, American expertise in financial practices and church administration was shared with their African counterparts. The sharing of ideas is a two-way street. Similar exchanges are happening all over the world between partner conferences.

Second, there is a sharing of people. There are now more African persons serving churches in the Great Plains Conference than any other non-Anglo group of clergy. They are serving in small towns, in urban settings, and on the conference staff. There is a shortage of clergy in that conference, and the willingness of African clergy to serve these congregations is a blessing to the communities. The expertise of an African as the coordinator of mercy and justice ministries for the conference strengthened the three international mission partnerships that the conference has. Previous to that appointment, the presence of two pastors who were originally from Zimbabwe led to forming that mission partnership. The General Board of Global Ministries is recruiting persons in mission from a variety of different countries. Some are leaving Africa to come to the United States as missionaries, reversing the pattern that was common for most of the twentieth century. The Board's description has become "mission from everywhere to everywhere."

The third effect of global sharing is a common approach to our global mission of transforming the world. For several years The United Methodist Church was a significant participant in the effort to reduce the incidence of malaria in sub-Saharan Africa. While we raised a large amount of money, our partners viewed our on-the-ground network of churches, clinics, and schools as a key contribution to the global effort. I personally participated in the celebration that kicked off the distribution of bed nets in rural Zimbabwe, and it was the church's influence and partnership with the government in that district that helped the campaign be successful.

In the future of the Wesleyan movement, these aspects of our global sharing position us for maximum impact on the entire world. Changes in transportation, communication, culture, technology, and the movements of people suggest that the process of globalization is going to continue. A church that has a truly global identity will be best positioned for missional effectiveness in the future.

Mission Statement

Perhaps the most significant positive sign for the Wesleyan movement was the adoption of the mission statement in 1996. While this has been referenced at several points in this book, two crucial aspects are highlighted here.

First, the phrase "make disciples of Jesus Christ for the transformation of the world" is equivalent to the original Wesleyan mission of "reform the continent and spread scriptural holiness across the land." When early Wesleyans used the phrase "scriptural holiness," they meant the way of salvation taught in the Bible aiming at entire sanctification by grace through faith. By clarifying its mission in this way, The United Methodist Church reconnected with its origins and with its official doctrinal statements.

I wrote the first draft of the mission statement for a meeting of interested persons held in 1995. The draft statement recovered the eighteenth-century language of "spreading scriptural holiness." Gary Mueller, now bishop of the Arkansas Area, commented, "There aren't twenty people in American who know what that means. Let's quote Jesus instead." He suggested that the phrase from Matthew 28:19 was better because people understood it and because Jesus is more important than John Wesley. I had to agree. At the time the persons involved in drafting and supporting the mission statement knew that it would require twenty years to live into what it truly means. In some ways the last twenty years have seen wider acceptance of the phrase but also a slower understanding of how to apply it.

The second aspect is that clarity of purpose is essential for any organization experiencing disruption in its environment. For any business, there are always opportunities to lose focus and expend resources on many different possibilities. Successful businesses are those that know their key area of competence and are disciplined in being the best they can be at that task.

My wife, Mary Lou, is president of Reece Construction Co. They build concrete structures for highways such as bridges and culverts. Occasionally they have accepted work to pour sidewalks or to place specialized concrete to resist corrosion from chemicals. By and large these jobs did not go well because they did not truly fall in the company's area of expertise where it could meet the needs of the marketplace. Over time, they have come back to their main purpose of building concrete structures and have continued to be successful at it.

The future of the Wesleyan movement will come as it focuses on the mission of making disciples of Jesus Christ for the transformation of the world and aligns its resources to pursue excellence in that task. Having clarity about the mission is the first and most important step in pursuing that goal.

The Magnificent Future

On October 11, 1981, my father, S. Jameson Jones Jr., preached a sermon in Asheville, North Carolina, based on Romans 8:18-19. For this text, he preferred the translation by J. B. Phillips, which says, "In my opinion whatever we may have to go through now is less than nothing compared with the magnificent future God has planned for us. The whole creation is on tiptoe to see the wonderful sight of the sons [and daughters] of God coming into their own." Dad asked,

> Do you believe that? That God has a magnificent future for us? I do....
>
> I wonder about the power that would be released from Church Street in Asheville if we would really believe that God is calling us to live into that future—with courage, with commitment, with confidence, with a ministry that reaches out from these powerhouses of worship—becoming agents of change and transformation to make a better world.
>
> Let us live by that faith. Let us live by the power that God makes available to us. Let us bring to our mission a spirit of courage and confidence, knowing that God calls us, and empowers us, to do his will—even in our world today![4]

My father made the point in the sermon that this letter was written to a group of Christians living at the heart of the Roman Empire and already experiencing difficulties. Their descendants would worship in catacombs to hide from the authorities. Yet,

Paul could say that their present circumstances were nothing compared to what God has in store for God's people.

There is no doubt that the Wesleyan movement has been through better times than it is currently experiencing in America. Many persons have become discouraged over recent trends. Remember that it has not always been this way, and that with God's help and our faithfulness the future can truly be magnificent.

I've heard it said that "if genuine revival ever comes to America, it will come through the Methodists. They have done it before, if they will only remember it. They have the right doctrine if they will only preach it. And they have the right organization if they will only use it." I am not sure that such a revival will have to come through the Wesleyans. I find great hope and promise in a variety of Christian churches. However, I do believe that the Wesleyan movement has an important role to play in God's purposes, and I am excited to be a part of it, whatever form it takes.

Notes

1. The Magnificent Future from a Magnificent Past

1. "Thoughts upon Methodism," §§2, 4, and 8, in *The Works of John Wesley*, 9:527–29.

2. Charles Ferguson's history of American Methodism was titled *Organizing to Beat the Devil: Methodists and the Making of America* (Garden City, NY: Doubleday, 1971).

3. L. Gregory Jones, *Christian Social Innovation: Renewing Wesleyan Witness* (Nashville: Abingdon Press, 2016), 1–2.

4. J. Gregory Dees, "The Meaning of 'Social Entrepreneurship,'" Duke University, October 31, 1998, rev. May 30, 2001, https://entrepreneurship.duke.edu/news-item/the-meaning-of-social-entrepreneurship/.

5. Jones, *Christian Social Innovation*, 4.

6. Ibid., 5.

7. Ibid., 8, 12.

8. David J. Bosch, *Transforming Mission: Paradigm Shifts in*

Theology of Mission (Maryknoll, NY: Orbis Books, 1996), 52–53. The quotation in the last sentence is from Michael Singleton, "Obsession with Possession?" *Pro Mundi Vita: Africa Dossiers*, no. 4, (1977): 28.

9. Jones, *Christian Social Innovation*, 27–28.

10. The United Methodist Church, *The Book of Discipline of the United Methodist Church 2016* (Nashville: The United Methodist Publishing House, forthcoming).

11. Personal conversation.

12. Jones, *Christian Social Innovation*, 51.

13. Jaroslav Pelikan, *The Vindication of Tradition* (New Haven, CT: Yale University Press, 1986), 65.

2. Key Questions

1. Kavin Rowe, *World Upside Down: Reading Acts in the Graeco-Roman Age* (Oxford: Oxford University Press, 2009), 18.

2. Aristides, *Apology*, translated by D. M. Kay, http://www.earlychristianwritings.com/text/aristides-kay.html, retrieved October 2, 2016.

3. Rowe, *World Upside Down*, 140–41.

4. St. Andrew UMC, Plano, Texas, http://www.standrewumc.org/our-mission.

5. John Wesley, "Scriptural Christianity," §IV.3, in *The Works of John Wesley*, 1:174–75.

6. David Hempton, *Methodism: Empire of the Spirit* (New Haven, CT: Yale University Press, 2005), 19.

7. Nathan O. Hatch, *The Democratization of American Christianity* (New Haven, CT: Yale University Press, 1989), 3.

8. Robert D. Putnam, *Bowling Alone: The Collapse and Revival of American Community* (New York: Simon and Schuster, 2000), 287.

9. Ibid., 403, 408–9. I removed the italics that are in the original text.

10. Ibid., 410.

11. Moisés Naím, *The End of Power: From Boardrooms to Battlefields and Churches to States, Why Being in Charge Isn't What It Used to Be* (New York: Basic Books, 2014), 1.

12. Ibid., 54, 58.

13. Ibid.

14. Ibid., 64.

15. Ibid., 65.

16. Thomas L. Friedman, *The World Is Flat: A Brief History of the Twenty-First Century* (New York: Farrar, Straus and Giroux, 2005).

17. Kenda Creasy Dean, *Almost Christian: What the Faith of Our Teenagers Is Telling the American Church* (Oxford: Oxford University Press, 2010), 11–12.

18. Christian Smith with Melissa Lundquist Denton, *Soul-Searching: The Religious and Spiritual Lives of American Teenagers* (New York: Oxford University Press, 2005), 171.

19. Dean, *Almost Christian*, 14.

20. Ibid., 49.

21. Richard B. Wilke, *And Are We Yet Alive? The Future of The United Methodist Church* (Nashville: Abingdon Press, 1986), 9.

22. *The Book of Discipline of The United Methodist Church*

(Nashville: The United Methodist Publishing House, 1996), 114.

23. Gil Rendle, *Journey in the Wilderness: New Life for Mainline Churches* (Nashville: Abingdon Press, 2010), 1, 2.

24. John Wesley, "The Minutes, London Conference, June 1744," *The Works of John Wesley*, 10:124.

3. Doctrine, Spirit, and Discipline

1. "Thoughts upon Methodism," in *The Works of John Wesley*, 9:527, 530.

2. *The Book of Discipline*, 262. Deacons are asked the first two questions as well.

3. Scott J. Jones, *United Methodist Doctrine: The Extreme Center* (Nashville: Abingdon Press, 2002), 47.

4. *The Book of Discipline*, ¶120, 91.

5. The United Methodist Church, *Call to Action: Steering Team Report* (Nashville: Abingdon Press, 2010), 8; see http://s3.amazonaws.com/Website_Properties/connectional-table/documents/call-to-action-steering-team-report.pdf.

6. *Minutes of Several Conversations Between the Rev. Thomas Coke, LL.D., the Rev. Francis Asbury and others . . . composing a Form of Discipline for the Ministers, Preachers and other Members of the Methodist Episcopal Church in America* (Philadelphia: Charles Cist, 1785), 4.

7. John Wesley, "The Means of Grace," §II.1, in *The Works of John Wesley*, 1:381.

8. "The Character of a Methodist," §12, in *The Works of John Wesley*, 9:39.

9. See *The Book of Discipline*, ¶101, 43.

10. Scott Jones, "20 Components of an Evangelistically Effective Congregation," http://extremecenter.com/documents/20-components-of-an-effectively-evangelistic-church/.

11. John Wesley, "Upon Our Lord's Sermon on the Mount, IV," in *The Works of John Wesley*, 1:533–34.

12. Dick Wills, *Waking to God's Dream: Spiritual Leadership and Church Renewal* (Nashville: Abingdon Press, 1999).

13. Noor Wazwaz, "It's Official: The U.S. Is Becoming a Minority-Majority Nation," *U.S. News and World Report*, July 6, 2015, http://www.usnews.com/news/articles/2015/07/06/its-official-the-us-is-becoming-a-minority-majority-nation.

14. Fred Dews, "What Percentage of U.S. Population is Foreign Born?" Brookings, October 3, 2013, https://www.brookings.edu/blog/brookings-now/2013/10/03/what-percentage-of-u-s-population-is-foreign-born/.

15. *The Book of Discipline*, ¶101, 43.

4. Discarded Baggage

1. *The Book of Discipline*, ¶47, 37.

2. The United Methodist Church, *Call to Action: Steering Team Report* (Nashville: Abingdon Press, 2010), 9; see http://s3.amazonaws.com/Website_Properties/connectional-table/documents/call-to-action-steering-team-report.pdf.

3. Ibid.

4. L. Gregory Jones, *Christian Social Innovation: Renewing Wesleyan Witness* (Nashville: Abingdon Press, 2016), 24–25.

5. A Future with Hope

1. Scott J. Jones and Arthur D. Jones, *Ask: Faith Questions in a Skeptical Age* (Nashville: Abingdon Press, 2015).

2. *The Book of Discipline,* ¶601, 394.

3. The United Methodist Church, *Call to Action: Steering Team Report* (Nashville: Abingdon Press, 2010), 8; see http://s3.amazonaws.com/Website_Properties/connectional-table/documents/call-to-action-steering-team-report.pdf.

4. Jameson Jones, *The Magnificent Future: Messages of Hope for the Church*, ed. L. Gregory Jones (Durham, NC: Glenmore Press, 1983), 131–32.

CPSIA information can be obtained
at www.ICGtesting.com
Printed in the USA
LVOW04s1140111016

508194LV00003B/3/P